WRITING IN THE ELECTRONIC ENVIRONMENT: ELECTRONIC TEXT AND THE FUTURE OF CREATIVITY AND KNOWLEDGE

by

IAN A. COLFORD

Halifax
Nova Scotia
1996

...mation Studies

Occasional Paper 59

The Occasional Papers series of the School of Library and Information Studies, Dalhousie University, is a forum for the dissemination of refereed scholarly papers, bibliographies, checklists, symposia proceedings, and compilations of articles on topics of interest to a world-wide community of librarians and other information professionals. In addition, it is a forum for the encouragement of research in the field, for first-time authors and others whose practical contribution, innovation, or critical analysis merits recognition.

Completed manuscripts or proposals are welcomed for consideration by the Series Editor, Dr. Bertrum MacDonald. Instructions for authors can be obtained by writing to the editor at the School of Library and Information Studies.

A complete list of titles in this series is found at the back of this volume. Copies of Occasional Paper no. 59 can be ordered from:

The Director
School of Library and Information Studies
Dalhousie University
Halifax, Nova Scotia, Canada
B3H 3J5

OR

The Vine Press
c/o Mr. Eric Winter
The Library Association
7 Ridgmount Street
London, England
WC1E 7AE

Canadian Cataloguing in Publication Data

Colford, Ian.

Writing in the electronic environment

(Occasional papers series, ISSN 0318-7403; no. 59)

ISBN 0-7703-9770-0

1. Humanities -- Data processing. 2. Authorship -- Data processing. 3. Electronic publishing. I. Dalhousie University. School of Library and Information Studies. II. Title. III. Series: Occasional papers series (Dahouisie University. School of Library and Information Studies) ; no.59.

AZ105.C64 1996   001.3'0285'4   C95-950324-2

TO

the memory of

Dr. Horace Bernard Colford,

a man of compassion, grace, and wisdom

Table of Contents

Preface

There is every chance that the title of this volume appears excessively ambitious in its attempt to be comprehensive and brands my undertaking as impossibly challenging. I hope this is not the case because what I propose to deal with is in reality quite specific and, in some respects, rather narrow.

Within the context of the present volume the phrase "electronic text" will refer primarily, though not exclusively, to the creative work as it is being formulated and composed. It is a topic of great interest, one that has engaged artists and philosophers for hundreds of years. A multitude of books have been written about the creative process—enough to fill a small library—yet it remains a mystery. Questions abound: where does the creative impulse come from, how is the work conceived, what kinds of changes does it undergo in its journey from the abstract region of the brain to the physical terrain of the printed page? These are only a few, but they illustrate the point that there are no definitive answers available, at least to mere mortals. Few artists and writers would presume to have the answers. The creative process is as much a mystery to them as it is to the rest of us.

There can be no argument, however, that creativity exists—and has existed for thousands of years—and that certain individuals are endowed with the ability to render the human condition into art, creating extraordinary work that endures and that continues to touch us even after a great deal of time has elapsed. I am not going to discuss the process itself. Rather, I wish to consider the various means by which the writer's ideas and passions find their way into the physical realm where we can access them on the printed page.

Historically, the practice of expressing oneself, whether orally or in writing, has been influenced by technology, and "technology" can be interpreted as broadly or, one suspects, as narrowly as one wishes. For those linguists and anthropologists who have spent decades exploring the origins of human communication, language itself is a "technology." The printing press is most certainly a "technology." However, all of this serves only as background for my focus of attention throughout this volume: the electronically stored text in as many of its manifestations as my limited experience allows me to envision. My reading has been firmly grounded in the humanities, and I intend to discuss electronic text almost exclusively from a humanities point of view. I have no wish to delve into technical matters of which I have a less than adequate understanding. Nor do I intend to examine how the wizardry of computer engineers has made it possible for us to watch our words dance across a screen and re-arrange or obliterate themselves at our command. Rather, I wish to consider how we as humans respond to this relatively young electronic medium—how it affects our thoughts and certain of our behaviours, and our creative imagination. I will then move on to a few social ramifications having mostly to do with libraries and issues of storage and retrieval and the concept of collective memory. Finally, I hope to provide a few cogent observations regarding the future that we will all share.

Acknowledgement

I am grateful to everyone who read this manuscript in its various stages of completion for their insightful comments, especially my wife Collette. I would also like to thank Dr. William Birdsall for suggesting the topic and for recommending approval of the six-month special leave that made it possible for me to engage in research and complete the initial draft. As well, I am grateful to Bertrum MacDonald for his meticulous reading of the manuscript.

1

Introduction: A Humanist's View

> Turning and turning in the widening gyre
> The falcon cannot hear the falconer;
> Things fall apart; the centre cannot hold;
> Mere anarchy is loosed upon the world...
>
> W.B. Yeats "The Second Coming"

I do not cite Yeats to serve notice of anarchic bloodletting, but simply to introduce the theme of revolution—of radical and profound change—that brings with it new ways of thinking and of doing things. Yeats had turned his mind to something quite distinct from modes of human communication, but still, his words may illustrate a point.

Any kind of revolution—and the revolution may take place overnight or over the course of many decades or centuries and thus be perceived as more gradual or evolutionary—leaves carnage in its wake, even—or perhaps especially—one of a technological nature. With luck the damage will be minimal and will be outweighed by the benefits, which accrue in the form of change. If the changes wrought by our revolution actually hold and become part of the social order, this is because in some way the common good is being served: the changes make possible an activity, or lend an advantage, that could previously only be the object of dreams and speculation.

The revolutionary nature of electronic text is a theme that permeates the literature. There is no disputing the fact that in the last forty years computers have affected the lives of those of us inhabiting advanced societies in ways that only science fiction writers and futurologists could have imagined. Being able to access our own bank accounts through what appears to be an electronic window is only one not even very significant way, though it is certainly one of the more visible as automatic tellers proliferate and alter the landscape in which we live. However, it is likely that these machines do affect us more profoundly than we may at first imagine by modifying our concept of money from something remote and inaccessible to something that is readily and instantly available, at any time, in any place. Can there be any question that this sort of conceptual transformation changes how we behave?

The effects of electronic text may well be less apparent, and no doubt will be slower to take place, but they are certain to occur, if those who are writing on the subject these days are to be believed. Already we can identify some changes that have encroached upon the public domain. Anyone can purchase the complete works of Shakespeare on compact disk, take it home, and read it on their personal computer.

Bibliographic databases and encyclopedias in compact disk format have multiplied in a fashion that hardly seems rational, and there are but few libraries remaining that lack CD-ROM workstations for their patrons' use. Strictly speaking, CD-ROMS are electronic text only in the sense that they originate from an electronic source and require electronic equipment in order to be decoded: they are "second-generation" electronic text. But they can be easily converted back. The works of writers from the past, such as Jane Austen and Samuel Taylor Coleridge, are available in electronic format, usually on floppy disk, from mainstream academic publishers such as Oxford University Press. As well, contemporary works of literature are being "created" specifically for use on the computer: hypertext fictions that explode the myth that stories must be linear in construction, must have an identifiable beginning point, a middle, and a conclusion that wraps it all up. In some cases these works incorporate other media such as sound and image, both still and moving, into the text—and some hypertexts even solicit comments and contributions from the reader which then become part of the text, thus challenging the accepted notion of seemingly familiar concepts such as "story" and "text," "author," and "reader."

These are only a few of the recent developments that I will be discussing in this volume. The future of computerized activity in the humanities presents us with an abundance of possibilities. Who really knows where such things as electronic text will take us in the next fifty or one hundred years? To some, this future is inviting, a stimulus to creative activity. To others it may appear somewhat intimidating, a cross to bear. Either way, this future will soon be here, and whatever form it takes will be the reality each of us will face every day.

In order to gain some perspective on the future—and, indeed, on the present as well—I propose to take a look backward into the past, to see how we happened to arrive at this point in time, electronically speaking.

Human history has been largely a story of discovery, an account of successive technological innovations building one upon the other. The human mind is unique in its capacity to forge connections, to place disparate elements side by side and emerge with something radical and different: revolutionary. We have been living with the fruits of various discoveries for many years, and it is therefore difficult to cast our minds backward in an attempt to imagine what it may have been like for our ancestors to live at a time when certain of the accessories of daily life that we take for granted did not exist. It is perhaps much more difficult to go further back and try to imagine what life was like before the development of speech or writing. However, this is precisely what a number of theorists have busied themselves doing in an effort to unearth the link between language and behavior.

Civilization is really a process of information transfer. To have a society you need a code of conduct, and to have a code of conduct you must first develop a means of communication, so that the code will be uniform throughout society. We are accustomed to seeing our rules and regulations in written form. There may be room for interpretation, but everyone starts with an identical text. In a society that has not developed a written form of language to correspond with the verbal, spoken words are the text from which each individual interpretation springs. If we in our literate society confer a certain esteem upon our written language—mentally endowing it with a capacity to dictate our behaviour and, in essence, rule our lives—we must, by inference, conclude that members of a pre-literate, or oral, culture revered the spoken word in much the same way. Today, in our media-saturated culture, spoken language is often a disposable commodity and nothing more than garbage. Though always used as a means of information transfer, the nature of the information itself is occasionally suspect: when it is empty babble or when it is deliberately misleading. We can only presume this was not the case in oral cultures—presume, because without conclusive evidence how can we be sure of anything? And because the pre-literate society leaves no written record, this evidence is obviously lacking.

Walter J. Ong has much to say on this subject:

> Fully literate persons can only with great difficulty imagine what a primary oral culture is like, that is, a culture with no knowledge whatsoever of writing or even of the possibility of writing. Try to imagine a culture where no one has ever "looked up" anything. In a primary oral culture, the expression "to look up something" is an empty phrase: it would have no conceivable meaning. Without writing, words as such have no visual presence, even when the objects they represent are visual. They are sounds. (31)

I think it is reasonable to assume that the development of writing systems enabled people to formulate and give expression to thoughts of greater complexity and subtlety than was possible before such systems existed. What are the ramifications of such an assumption? Consider the mythmaker or "storyteller" in the pre-literate culture. If, as I suggested earlier, members of an oral society invest the spoken word with a reverence similar to that with which we regard the written word, then the storyteller becomes the living receptacle of that culture's collective memory. Those concerned with the survival of the oral traditions of the pre-literate culture, regardless of their social position or role, embody government, religion, law, history, custom, education, literature: all those facets of society that require language in order to get their meaning across. We hear it said today that information is power. Imagine the degree of power concentrated within the individual or individuals whose word, in essence, *was* law. Since these people were the fount of all knowledge, who would have the audacity to question what was being said? Indeed, who would even suspect that what was being said *could* be questioned?

The political implications of such a system of governance are obvious, at least from our jaundiced twentieth-century point of view. But what of culture, poetry, literature? In a pre-literate society in which words were not uttered frivolously or needlessly, it is likely that all facets of language as a tool for communication were employed in maintaining order and stability, in keeping enemies at bay, in ensuring the survival of the tribe—ongoing tasks that benefit from the unimpeded flow of information. It is therefore reasonable to assume that "literature" was a means of information transfer like any other. The "literary merit" of any utterance would be an alien concept in a society in which the successful transfer of information could mean life instead of death, survival instead of extinction. If consideration were ever given to the mode of transfer above and beyond the content of the message, it would be only to assess the effectiveness of the method.

It is possible that the development of a writing system lends a nation or community a certain advantage over others and makes the survival of its people, as well as the survival of their culture, more likely than it would have been without that system. Of course, there are cultures which, even today, have not developed a written heritage and which have survived and flourished over long periods. The works of Ruth Finnegan and Jack Goody, both of whom have spent years observing isolated pre-literate societies in Africa, bear this out. However, these societies remain at a relatively primitive stage of development, not having made any significant technological or political advances for many years.

Are we safe assuming that writing and literacy bring with them momentous changes that impinge upon all aspects of society? It is well known that when writing was being introduced to ancient Greece, as Plato records in his *Phaedrus*, Socrates warned, not only that this new technology would lead to an atrophy of the mind and erode the human capacity for thinking and recall, but also that once it is set down, the written message "drifts all over the place, getting into the hands not only of those who understand it, but equally of those who have no business with it" (Plato XXV). Maybe he was wrong about the nature of the change and the degree of danger, but what Socrates anticipated was surely a decisive and profound transformation, a departure from past practice on a major scale, and it still seems appropriate to believe that the introduction of something as fundamental as writing, which has the potential to permeate society and touch it at every level, would cause profound transformations to take place. However, as with any new technology, it did not drop out of the sky. It had to originate somewhere, engendered by a perceived need, developed because pressures came to bear that required attention, because a problem demanded a solution. In her book *Literacy and Orality: Studies in the Technology of Communication*, Ruth Finnegan argues against the kind of technological determinism that regards technology "as autonomous, that is as itself self-standing and independent of social shaping and as more or less inescapably determining social forms and relationships" (Finnegan 10).

The technological determinist assumes that once literacy (or some other technology) has been introduced, certain consequences will follow, as surely as night follows day. The problem with this view is that it seriously diminishes the role both society and the individual play in governing their own fate. The technological determinist "sees the technology as the crucial factor, as bringing with it a series of social consequences at every level. It affects 'society' as a whole, industry, organizations, social interaction, mental processes, and even our own view of ourselves as human beings"(Finnegan 10).

A more balanced view might take into account the idea that for thousands of years human beings have been adept at exploiting the environment to ensure their survival and, as long as survival was guaranteed, to take advantage of whatever tools lay about at their disposal and to devise other tools that would provide comfort and make life easier. At a time when human energy could be safely given over to leisure activities, the development of writing systems seems a reasonable technological progression. Before the establishment of permanent settlements, when all humans shared an uncertain, nomadic, tribal existence, where would the impetus to create a written record of their culture come from? For the impulse to do this to even exist is almost unthinkable, first of all because simple survival was the paramount concern for everyone, but also because it was impractical, given the fact that tribes drifted from one location to another depending on external factors such as the availability of food, weather patterns, territorial conflicts, etc. Even if the tools for writing had existed, why would people eking out a precarious, marginal existence in a hostile environment even want to write anything down? They would not want to burden themselves with written records when survival depended on moving quickly from place to place, and they would probably not want to leave such records behind if they were unlikely to revisit the site where the records were stored. Once the environment had been mastered and everyday life had become less uncertain, the possibility of sedentary activities such as writing seem much more plausible. The earliest cave paintings are probably a sign that nomadic life was coming to an end and that humans had acquired both the impulse and the means to leave behind a record of their existence.

There are factors to consider, then, besides the simple introduction of the technology of literacy into society. Writing, like any other tool, was fashioned by humans for a purpose. That it spread and that it helped to stabilize and perpetuate the culture of those societies whose members recognized its potential cannot be disputed. But the process by which humans made the transition from oral to literate beings is by no means clear.

As Anthony Smith puts it,

> It is easy when looking back at the affairs of the ancient world or of the Renaissance to see the techniques of writing and printing as autonomous phenomena "causing"—as if by their own free will—a series of discrete social effects. But technology is not an autonomous determinant of change. Rather, it is a convenient demarcator of change for the observer attempting to analyze a mass of interconnected events. (4)

"Writing in any medium is an act of appropriation. Writing pulls words or ideas out of their original time and stores them away for later use" (Bolter 42).

As Jay Bolter tells us, writing allows us to set our ideas down in order that we, or someone else, can consult and make use of them at a later date. Writing is also preservation, in the sense that the wisdom of the elders, the divinations of the prophets, the teachings of the sages, whatever, can be saved for posterity. Writing thus frees the human memory from the task of storing the vast accumulated wisdom of many centuries. For, in the pre-literate society, how else can knowledge be retained except in the memory? How else can information be passed down except orally? This line of questioning eventually leads to, of all things, the invention of poetry, or, more pedantically, the construction of word patterns around structured thought.

How does the tribal mythmaker in the pre-literate society, whose responsibility is the custodianship of tribal lore, pack so much information into his or her memory? And how is this information retrieved? The answer, according to Ong and Jan Vansina and others, is that information was stored in the memory using familiar formulas, or mnemonic structures. For us, some of the easiest things to recall—and the recollection is usually instantaneous—are, to take some examples, the cliché ("It was a dark and stormy night"), the simplistic maxim ("An apple a day..."), the idiomatic saying ("fit as a fiddle"), or the slogan or catchphrase ("Never give a sucker an even break"). These word patterns are so deeply embedded in our conscious memories that we could not forget them even if we wanted to. What better tool, then, for the storage and retrieval of lengthy and complex pieces of information than a series of equally cloying but unforgettable word patterns? Of course, the mythmaker (or tribal genealogist, or shaman, or high-priest, or medicine man, or praise singer) would probably have little reason to recall this information when alone. The information would be there, ready to be used, but since the initial reason for storing the information was to pass it to others, the individual entrusted with the preservation of tribal lore would in all likelihood require an audience to stimulate the memory, to draw the pertinent information forth and separate it from that which was not relevant. Because the object of any recital was to compel audience members to listen and to retain as much of what they were being told as possible, the orator would presumably stay close to the "original" formula—making use of language structures, such as rhythm, repetition, and rhyme, that act as mnemonic aids to retention—in order to get the message across effectively and to help the lesson adhere in the minds of listeners more or less intact.

Vansina maintains that "preliterate peoples have highly developed powers of memory, and hand down their traditions in a form made suitable for oral transmission by use of rhyme or other formula for linking the material together" (4).

Walter Ong takes this notion one step further, postulating a direct link between the mnemonic technique of recollection and the thought patterns of those who rely upon oral modes of communication for cultural stability.

> In a primary oral culture, to solve effectively the problem of retaining and retrieving carefully articulated thought, you have to do your thinking in mnemonic patterns, shaped for ready oral recurrence. Your thoughts must come into being in heavily rhythmic, balanced patterns, in repetitions or antitheses, in alliterations and assonances, in epithetic and other formulary expressions, in standard thematic settings...in proverbs which are constantly heard by everyone so that they come to mind readily and which themselves are patterned for retention and ready recall, or in other mnemonic form. (Ong 34)

Given the prevalence of the written word in all its forms which we encounter daily, we can perhaps be forgiven for losing touch with the oral roots of language. It is true, however, that in its oral incarnation, language is at its most powerful. We are reminded of this from time to time when we hear of a political leader mobilizing the citizenry of an entire nation, an evangelist convincing the lame that they can walk, a poet moving an audience of thousands to tears and laughter, all with the power of the spoken word.

Linguists and anthropologists, such as Ong and Jack Goody, trace the origins of Western literature to an oral tradition, arguing that the two works attributed to Homer, the *Iliad* and the *Odyssey*, rather than being discrete and internally cohesive works that issued from the creative imagination of a single writer, are more than likely amalgams of various oral texts that evolved and came together over many centuries until the development of written language enabled some Greek scribe to take them down as they were being dictated, thus preserving them in a form similar to that which they currently hold (Ong 17-30). Embedded in these two texts are elements that indicate a strong didactic impulse behind their composition: historical paradigms, instructions for social rituals, lessons in moral conduct. The stories and characters make the poems interesting as works of literature, but a prescriptive moral design remains very much on the surface.

The impulse and the ability to convey information are features that all animals, and possibly all life forms, share. It is basic to survival since few organisms live in total isolation. However, humans are the only creatures to leave behind a visual representation of their thoughts and feelings. Early writing systems tended to rely upon a direct pictorial representation of the object, situation, or series of events under discussion. However, the disadvantage of this kind of system becomes apparent the minute you try to give expression to abstract concepts. There is no way to convey messages that are not immediately tangible or rooted in everyday life. The invention of the alphabet, which either occurred in Greece around 750 BC or which can be attributed to the Western Semites 750 years prior to that (Goody 40), was the stride forward that liberated human thought from the purely temporal realm and allowed us to interpret as well as depict our surroundings. This was the beginning of phonetic writing, which evolved from picture writing. Phonetic writing is a system in which each letter, or symbol, corresponds not to a thing, but to a sound. In phonetic writing systems there is no longer a one-to-one correlation between the written symbol and the object being described. Instead, the written symbols refer to a system of sounds from which the reader is left to draw meaning and make connections to the visible world or to a conjectural world, the world of the author's mind. Jay Bolter calls phonetic representation a writing system "of the second order" because it places the reader at a secondary remove from the object of the written word (Bolter 47-49). It demands of the reader an ability to conceptualize, to construct in the mind a visual image of something that is not necessarily present. Phonetic writing also marks the beginning of language, which—as complex and multi-layered as it has become—is little more than a tacit contract among individuals that *this* set of symbols and *those* particular sounds constitute the most effective way to make each other understood. In order for members of a society to participate fully in the activities of that society, they must first be initiated into the language—taught the proper set of written symbols and also the sounds to which they correspond. To the uninitiated, and considered apart from the language of which they are perhaps the most vital component, the written symbols convey nothing, are merely marks, random and enigmatic. However, regarded within the context of the entire system—symbol, sound, and meaning—there is no limit to the messages these symbols can convey, no boundary that meaning cannot cross.

It is quite possible that writing altered the way people organized knowledge and even changed the way they thought. Free of the necessity to commit large blocks of information to memory, they could reach outward and actively engage their minds with ideas of a more intricate and abstract nature; they could reach inward and develop a self-conscious awareness. The assumption is that writing triggered a reconfiguration of the relationship between the human individual and his or her environment. There was a cognitive shift, a sighting of something beyond the immediate, both within and without. Of course, none of this happened instantaneously, as if a light had been switched on dispelling the primitive murk of the pre-literate world. Rather, changes occurred over time, over hundreds of years, as more people were introduced to writing and as the systems themselves evolved and grew in complexity and sophistication.

Jack Goody's work on the transition from oral to literate culture is of particular interest because he gives eloquent voice to the notion that the effects of writing upon human thinking and expression are both profound and inevitable. These effects are also deeply embedded within the societies in which they take hold because they touch upon the many ways in which humans communicate and develop their social nature.

> Systems of communication are clearly related to what man can make of his world both internally in terms of thought and externally in terms of his social and cultural organization. So the changes in the means of communication are linked in direct as well as indirect ways to changes in the patterns of human interaction. (Goody 3)

Goody also stresses that the introduction of a writing system into a culture that previously had no knowledge of writing has had a demonstrable impact on human modes of processing information and thus on how human individuals perceive the world around them and how they express those perceptions. Reporting on the anthropologist Reder's field work in West Africa studying the Vai language, Goody states that

> the evidence shows that the capacity to read changes those internal representations of language that mediate speech. This is a remarkable contention since it indicates that by

providing a visual component to language, writing alters not only the external models or maps...but also the internal ones, that is to say, it alters them in ways that feed back to the structures of speech and of perception. (268-9)

Stevan Harnad has identified "three revolutions in the history of human thought": the development of speech, the development of writing systems, and the invention of moveable type. These three phenomena are equated in his understanding because they represent the three instances in which human thought processes underwent significant qualitative transformation (Harnad, "Post-Gutenberg Galaxy" 39). Harnad's claim in this 1991 essay is that electronic text, combined with communication systems that promise almost instantaneous contact between individuals separated by enormous physical distances, represents a change of equal magnitude.

There can be no question that all knowledge to which we can claim possession was passed down to us in written form. The diversity of "writing spaces" employed over the centuries represents attempts to preserve this knowledge, and some performed this function more successfully than others. Egyptian stone and Sumerian clay tablets have survived for thousands of years. Yet the flexibility and portability of papyrus eventually made this the writing space of choice, even though its "shelf life" was much shorter. The Greeks and Romans adopted papyrus from the Egyptians and created "books" in the form of scrolls which consisted of sheets of papyrus glued end to end.

Each roll, 20 to 25 feet in length, held much less text than a modern book, so that longer works, such as the Homeric poems, had to be stored on many rolls. The roll later became a structural unit in writing, and Greek and Roman authors often conceived and wrote their works in units appropriate to the roll. (Bolter 38)

One drawback of the scroll format was that the technology failed to give accessibility the attention it deserved. None of our standard access tools—page numbers, indices, tables of contents—were being used in any systematic or consistent fashion. The next major technological innovation—what we recognize today as the paged book, or codex— originated in the second and third centuries A.D., and this technology provided an opportunity to solve some of the problems associated with access. It was also more compact and, hence, more portable (Bolter 38).

Prior to the mid-fifteenth century, when Gutenberg invented moveable type and built the first printing press, the duplication of important texts was a laborious and imposing task. Often relegated to monks, who had plenty of time and who regarded the duplication of sacred works as an act of penance, or sometimes to paid scribes, copying demanded long stretches of wakeful diligence of its practitioners. For this reason—and others, principally the expense and scarcity of the materials, such as vellum or parchment, involved in the production process—books were rare and costly, and the ability to read rarer still. The common individual had no recourse but to look to those who could read for instruction and enlightenment. The literate elite included the clergy, whose interests were served by keeping people ignorant and suitably in awe of

God's word as related in the scriptures, and the well-to-do, in whose service most commoners, or peasants, toiled all their lives and whose interests were thereby served by seeing that people remained simple and uneducated. With few exceptions during the centuries comprising the Middle Ages and for much of the Medieval period, the ability to read and write remained the exclusive domain of these two groups (Burke 102 ff).

Also at this time the vast majority of texts that were copied and distributed were sacred works, works handed down from ancient Greek or Latin sources, legal texts and records which codified the law of the land, and deeds and other such documents that made it possible for people to demonstrate their ownership of farms and estates and other property. Very few original works—that is, creative works or works representing radical breakthroughs in philosophical discourse—were being composed at this time, sacred or secular. The authority attributed to the written word (much the same as that attributed to the spoken word in oral cultures) was almost absolute simply because it was generally regarded as a mysterious, arcane, perhaps even divine object. "Authors," therefore, were by no means contemporary individuals who could be questioned about their work in the way we see writers interviewed on TV talk-shows. An author was in a very real sense an authority, a highly learned, possibly god-like, probably dead individual whose words were not normally subject to question. Of course there were works being written down, probably dictated to scribes—in England *Beowulf* and *Sir Gawain and the Green Knight* come to mind, in Iceland, for instance, the sagas—but in almost all cases these works were recorded and distributed anonymously, attributable to no one. And these works, like the Homeric epics, were most likely adapted from oral precursors which evolved over many generations.

However, when writing began to encroach upon the everyday lives of common people, an obstacle to the widespread endorsement of written works was a simple lack of trust. For those living on the land, toiling with their hands from daybreak to sundown all their lives, the only repository of local tradition, the only reliable record of past events, existed in the memories of elders in the community. In order, for example, to verify a land claim or to establish whether an heir had attained his majority, or perhaps recall when a battle or natural disaster had taken place, it was customary to consult an elderly person whose memory could be trusted and ask for an account of the past in relation to the question at hand. If the question had legal ramifications, statements would be made on oath before a tribunal. For those who traditionally had depended upon oral testimony to establish precedent, written documents probably offered little reassurance. Because it was new, documentary evidence (incomprehensible squiggles on paper if you were illiterate, and most people were) must have at first appeared suspect and flimsy compared to the statements of witnesses.

> Documents did not immediately inspire trust. As with other innovations in technology, there was a long and complex period of evolution, particularly in the twelfth century in England, before methods of production were developed which proved acceptable both to traditionalists and to experts in literacy. There was no straight and simple line of

progress from memory to written record. People had to be persuaded—and it was difficult to do—that documentary proof was a sufficient improvement on existing methods to merit the extra expense and mastery of novel techniques which it demanded. (Clanchy 294)

If, as Anthony Smith maintains, "Writing transformed knowledge into information," (6) then printing made it possible to easily duplicate that information and distribute it wherever passable roads or waterways existed.

There has been much discussion about Gutenberg and about the invention of printing in fifteenth-century Europe and its possible effects upon patterns of human communication. However, living in a culture dominated by print, our only experience of scribal culture comes to us in printed form. We are hardly in a position to make conclusive declarations regarding the lengthy and complex process that was the transition to print. Any statements we do make must of necessity be theoretical and speculative in nature.

It does seem clear, however, that the technology of print was generally regarded as an improvement over previous methods of document production, else it would not have taken such firm hold of the popular imagination and so easily squeezed manuscript books to the periphery of the market. Most theorists seem to agree that at least two features of the period after the invention of printing, and before the absolute dominance of print, played a significant role in relegating manuscripts to the sideline of history. These are 1) the rapid spread of the technology, first within Germany and then throughout the rest of Europe, and 2) the sheer number of volumes printed during the first fifty or so years that the technology was available.

Two of the most obvious advantages of the printed over the handwritten process of producing texts are the relative ease, and the accuracy, of duplication. In an era when the production of a new text could take months of concentrated effort by a scribe, books were as rare as the ability to read them. Those who did not live close to a centre of learning might never come into contact with any form of writing their entire lives. The new process of printing using movable type meant that identical documents could be produced in large quantities in a short time. More texts meant that more people would be exposed to the printed word, which would stimulate the desire for learning and the spread of literacy, which would in turn result in an increased demand for books. Granted, this did not occur overnight. Febvre and Martin place the "arrival" of the printed book on a large scale sometime in the first decade of the sixteenth century, between 1500 and 1510. They report that "Little by little it displaced the manuscript in library collections, relegating it to second place, and by 1550 the latter was hardly used, except by scholars for special purposes" (Febvre and Martin 262).

Within a hundred years after the invention of printing, then, manuscripts had become obsolete, a pedagogical curiosity.

It has been noted that early printers attempted to mimic the appearance of the manuscript page with their printed page, presumably because they felt their customers would be more comfortable confronting a commodity that resembled something with which they were already familiar, or possibly because they were not yet prepared to accept that the appearance of a book could diverge from what was widely considered standard or customary. The procedures had changed radically, yet in the first years "handwork and presswork continued to appear almost indistinguishable, even after the printer had begun to depart from scribal conventions and to exploit some of the new features inherent in his art" (Eisenstein 51). However, more important than the appearance of the page is the accuracy of the text, and here also the new process proved a significant advancement over the old. Scribal duplication was always prone to error, even with the most diligent copyists to be found. And there was the chance too that in cases where an original offered more than one possible reading—because of smudges or inferior work or linguistic ambiguity—that a scribe might endeavour to improve on the original in order to make the meaning more clear. This is associated with the whole issue of preservation, because, as Elizabeth Eisenstein notes, "No manuscript, however useful as a reference guide, could be preserved for long without undergoing corruption by copyists" (113-4). She identifies a phenomena called "textual drift" in which subsequent copies strayed further and further from the original, in the sense that errors were introduced and compounded and passed along as copies were made from copies. Documents that were in demand were never safe from a variety of dangers, even from well-meaning scribes.

> Insofar as records were seen and used, they were vulnerable to wear and tear. Stored documents were vulnerable to moisture and vermin; theft and fire. However they might be collected or guarded within some great message center, their ultimate dispersal and loss was inevitable. To be transmitted by writing from one generation to the next, information had to be conveyed by drifting texts and vanishing manuscripts. (Eisenstein 114)

Printing allowed texts to be easily and accurately duplicated, and this is Gutenberg's primary contribution to western culture. But what of the materials being printed? Who was making the decision to produce one book instead of another?

In the early years of print the actual texts being reproduced were not new works but those which already existed in manuscript form, and it is not difficult to see why. Printers were businessmen. They were motivated to manufacture and assemble their printed texts not out of community largesse or a wish to influence the course of history but, very simply, to turn a profit. The books they decided to produce with the new technology were those that had proven popular in manuscript form and for which a ready audience already existed. Sales would be assured. Little risk was involved, and from a commercial standpoint, this is good business.

> Like their modern counterparts, 15th-century publishers only financed the kind of book they felt sure would sell enough copies to show a profit in a reasonable time. We should not therefore be surprised to find that the immediate effect of printing was merely to

further increase the circulation of those works which had already enjoyed success in manuscript, and often to consign other less popular texts to oblivion. (Febvre and Martin 249)

Print did not immediately stimulate the production of new or original works of literature or of scientific learning or of philosophy. What it did do, however, was make the works of the ancient philosophers, astronomers, poets, historians, and rhetoricians more widely available than ever before. It may be true, as Clanchy argues, that "lay literacy grew out of bureaucracy rather than from any abstract desire for education or literature" (19), but the pursuit of knowledge is something else again, and it was directly influenced by what was available to be studied. In the early days of print, knowledge was not so much being discovered as it was being rediscovered (Eisenstein 124).

The idea of the author as unquestioned authority likely began to lose favour as the learning of the ancients was circulated wherever printing shops were established, coming into the hands of many people, and not just those who accepted such pronouncements unconditionally. As availability of the technology spread, people began writing their own books, formulating new ideas, challenging the old. With living authors in their midst, readers discovered that the ideas recorded on the printed page were not "cast in stone" and could actually be discussed and debated, discovered as well that they could question the validity of those ideas and quite possibly disagree with them. While still held in high esteem, the older classical writings were subject to the same close scrutiny "as ancient sages were retrospectively cast in the role of authors—prone to human error" (Eisenstein 122). People wrote commentaries on popular works. The complexion of the learning industry altered as methods of teaching began to emphasize interrogation rather than blind respect, empirical experimentation rather than submissive acceptance.

Once printing had taken hold and achieved widespread sanction as the most convenient and sensible means of preserving knowledge about the past and the present, mnemonic formulae were no longer called upon to serve a strictly utilitarian role as an aid to passing information from one generation to the next. Important information or instructions could be written down and easily copied. There was no longer any need to dress the language up in ways that would ease the burden of memorization.

> Cadence and rhyme, images and symbols ceased to fulfill their traditional function of preserving the collective memory. Technical information could be conveyed directly by plain words, unambiguous numbers, diagrams and maps. The aesthetic experience became increasingly autonomous and the function of works of art had to be redefined. (Eisenstein 125)

Changes of a much more subtle nature in the way the printed page could have affected those who came into contact with it have been proposed by Marshall McLuhan in *The Gutenberg Galaxy*, his groundbreaking and still controversial book from 1962. In his discussion, McLuhan stresses the role of the senses, visual and aural, in the absorption of knowledge. He points out that because of its abrupt arrival and ascendance, and the fact that it was a mechanized process based on order, regularity, and symmetry, print—much more so than handwriting—impressed itself upon the minds of readers and altered their visual understanding of, and approach to, the written word. Over time, as the mechanized process became more sophisticated and the texts themselves more expertly fashioned, the act of reading was isolated from its aural component. "The reader of print...stands in an utterly different relation to the writer from the reader of manuscript. Print gradually made reading aloud pointless, and accelerated the act of reading till the reader could feel 'in the hands of' his author" (125). Once free of the eccentricities of its written counterpart, the printed word made the act of reading itself less strenuous, required less of the reader in the way of simple effort. Because of the way it laid the words out on the page, the technology succeeded in making the printed word, and thus its meaning, more readily accessible to a growing population of readers. Also, since texts were more numerous, they could be held side by side and compared. This encouraged conformity of expression, the result being that language itself within national boundaries was fixed in the minds of the literate population as something that could be used properly or improperly, that functioned best when certain structural principles were applied. Correct usages were established. But McLuhan also extends the influence of the printed word to other facets of society, seeing it as a catalyst for changes that would not have come about had not print caused a psychic shift in people's minds, altering the way they perceived the world around them. "It cannot be easily grasped, else it had been explained long ago, that the mechanical principle of visual uniformity and repeatability which is inherent in the press steadily extended itself to include many kinds of organization" (209).

McLuhan's argument returns again and again to the idea of a strong "visual bias" within literate culture, "a bias derived from only one source, the phonetic alphabet" (108), a bias, furthermore, that was reinforced by the introduction of print. In her discussion of these theories, Elizabeth Eisenstein remarks that though "McLuhan's suggestion that scanning lines of print affected thought-processes is at first glance somewhat mystifying...further reflection suggests that the thoughts of readers are guided by the way the contents of books are arranged and presented. Basic changes in book format might well lead to changes in thought-patterns" (88).

Though difficult to prove, McLuhan's thesis that the impact of print was felt throughout society remains compelling, and though they did not appear immediately, the new printing technology did bring with it changes in temperament and habit that could never be reversed once they had taken hold. As James Burke rather sweepingly states, "Printing changed the entire, backward-looking view of society, with its stultifying respect for the achievements of the past, to one that looked forward to progress and improvement" (Burke 123). Ease of duplication may have put scribes out of work, but as we have seen it also made books more plentiful, more readily available than ever before. Books ceased to be objects of veneration in and of themselves and instead became subject to demand because of the information or entertainment they contained. And eventually this demand was filled by a willing supply of authors ready to advance new ideas. As the technology spread, the number of new works printed each year multiplied. Libraries were filled. Knowledge built upon knowledge. This process of accumulation helped stimulate the learning explosion in sixteenth-century Europe; it aided in the propagation of Reformation doctrine; and it played a major role in moulding the world in which we live. All of this is part of modern historical lore. But it would be presumptuous to refer to the influence of print only in the past tense. We still experience the effects of print technology every day, even as we move toward what some are calling a post-print age.

As far as the humanities are concerned, print, the proliferation of texts, the rise of the leisure class, and a growing demand for works that emerged from an aesthetic sensibility, led in part to the veneration of the author rather than the word and contributed to the romantic myth of the solitary, angst-ridden poet in his garret. For many years now the author has been the subject of a degree of critical scrutiny every bit as minute and exacting as that bestowed upon the work itself. Clues to the meaning of literary texts have been sought within the life of the author. In some critical circles the author and the text are considered inseparable, eternally linked in a relationship of cause and effect. In others, that opinion is reviled and exactly the opposite view is maintained. And in many respects it is the technology that has brought us to this impasse.

One point that has not yet been addressed but which is implicit throughout the discussion that follows is the complementarity of technologies of communication. We all know that the introduction of writing systems did not put an end to verbal intercourse. It was together with orality that writing formed the basis of a more complex and efficient communication system that made the delivery of elaborate and abstract concepts from one individual to another possible. Similarly, we can assume that the introduction of verbal communication in prehistoric societies did not render obsolete the use of hand gestures and facial expressions as means of communicating thoughts and feelings. Neither did the introduction of print technology mean that people stopped writing by hand with quills and fountain pens. Rather, the two technologies worked together to create a flexible and powerful infrastructure capable of spreading knowledge and disseminating information more widely than ever before. It therefore seems reasonable to assume that electronic technologies will not totally supersede print, writing, and all the rest, but will extend and augment the many capabilities of which we already make constant use. And presumably the result will be a system of communication that enables us to do things we already do but in a more efficient manner. In the face of hubris and assertions of superiority that sometimes accompany technological advancement it is helpful to remember that even in advanced societies gestures and facial expressions as very useful means of communication have yet to disappear.

What I wish to explore in the following pages is the new electronic medium which some regard as the logical successor to the print technology with which most of us are familiar. I will be touching upon a broad spectrum of topics. However, I intend to keep these firmly under control and steer them in a direction of interest to humanities specialists, creative writers, librarians, and those of us who are held in constant fascination by the word on the page.

2

The Variety of Electronic Texts

In as much as the theories of our predecessors proved variously defective and fallacious, so, it may be argued, are our guesses no better than those of old, and in turn they will go the way of all knowledge. Theories rise and fall as better, truer theories replace them; yet it is unwarranted to conclude that science is truth for a day. The essential truths endure; the stepping-stones within the same circle of validity have a permanent service, for they bear the stamp of a more rigid discipline.

Joseph Jastrow (*The Story of Human Error* 34)

Every new and good thing is liable to seem eccentric and perhaps dangerous at first glimpse, perhaps more than what is really eccentric, really irrelevant to life. And therefore we must always listen to the voice of eccentricity, within ourselves and in the world. The alien, the dangerous, like the negligible near thing, may seem irrelevant to purpose and yet the call to our own fruitful development. This does not mean that we should surrender to whatever novelty is brought to attention. It does mean that we must practice to some extent an imaginative surrender to every novelty that has even the most tenuous credentials.

Brewster Ghiselin ("Introduction" to *The Creative Process* 31)

It may seem a cliché stated thus, but "electronic text" is a phrase of which it can genuinely be said it means many things to many people. In the broadest sense, any meaningful symbols that are encoded as a sequence of digital impulses in a magnetic medium qualify as "electronic text." In order for us to make sense of text stored in this manner, we require an electronic device capable of retrieving the bits of data and translating them back into symbols, precisely as they existed before the encoding process took place. This device should also be capable of providing a visual display of these symbols, preferably in an orderly fashion, on a screen, or else deliver them as output to a printer.

It is a complex technology that performs all of these functions for us, but it is one that has become so widely available—one could almost say ubiquitous in a technologically advanced society—that we hardly give a moment's thought to the intricate network of wires, connectors, and chips that resides beyond the screen. Today, computers successfully conceal their complexity from us. And, in fact, most of us who encounter computers on a daily basis are content knowing nothing of how they operate. In the last five years or so, many of the refinements in computer technology have been of a quantitative rather than a qualitative nature. Machines are more powerful, faster, and easier to operate than they were yesterday—they can manipulate more data with greater ease and efficiency—but *what* they do has remained virtually unchanged for many years.

In this chapter I propose to look at a number of textual phenomena and provide a comprehensive sampling of what could be called "static" electronic text: electronic versions of literary and other standard works, networked communication and electronic journals, and, finally, hypertext. These products are "static" in much the same way that a book is passive and inert: we are invited as readers to open and examine them as closely as we may wish and derive whatever meaning we can. However, the authors of these texts neither expect nor encourage their readers to alter their work. That said, I must add the following caveat. In the world of computers and e-text, definitions tend to be fluid and categories are full of pitfalls. Both hypertext and electronic journals exist at the periphery of this group I have just described, each positioned very near the boundary marking the domain of the "active" or "interactive" electronic text.

Standard Texts

What good is an electronic text? What can you do with an electronic version of, say, Shakespeare's *Sonnets* that you cannot do with a printed version?

At first look, these questions may seem facetious in their simplicity. But the fact is that today there is a great deal of energy being expended, and a great many people being kept occupied, in a multitude of text-conversion projects that were initiated because someone saw an advantage in electronic versions of standard works. Reva Basch reports that the Georgetown Center for Text and Technology, which has been compiling a catalogue of electronic text projects, lists "over 300 such projects in almost 30 countries" (Basch 14). Clearly the perceived need for electronic text is widespread. And presumably those overseeing these projects believe that electronic texts are good, that they represent progress, assumptions that are quite likely valid. But once all the inputting is done and the projects are complete, what will we have that we never had before? What will e-texts do for us? What will we, as readers, gain?

One of the first, most widely-known and celebrated, e-text projects, initiated almost 20 years ago at Indiana University under the guidance of Michael Hart, is called Project Gutenberg. This project, which continues to this day, "began...as an experiment in the useful applications, values, and potential utility of mainframe computers" (Hart 6). From these broadly inclusive origins, Project Gutenberg developed into an effort "to encourage the creation and distribution of English-language electronic texts" (Hart 6). Hart expands on this, stating more specifically, "Our goals are to provide a collection of 10,000 of the most used books by the year 2000, and to reduce, and we do mean reduce, the effective costs to the user to a price of approximately one cent per book..." (Hart 7).

One advantage of amassing a huge inventory of e-texts, then, is a reduction in costs to the reader, who would presumably have access to all 10,000 texts for a single price. But Hart goes on: "These electronic books will not have to be rebound, reprinted, reshelved, etc. They will not have to be reserved and restricted to use by one patron at a time. All materials will be available to all patrons from all locations at all times" (Hart 7).

At the very basic physical level, then, electronic books, unlike traditional books, are not subject to the trauma that inevitably results from continued handling. Their binding does not weaken and crumble and eventually fail, leaving pages loose and liable to loss or damage. E-texts are also not subject to limited print runs, with the unavoidable result that editions go "out of print" and have to be reissued. E-texts save labour because nobody has to remove them from one physical location in order for them to be put to use in another. And finally, the number of copies of an electronic text that can be generated from a single source file is limited only by the number of people who wish to consult it. Reserve queues do not exist; where electronic texts are concerned there is no waiting.

These advantages are considerable. However, Hart is referring to a restricted category of texts: "10,000 of the most used books." This is of course laudable, but how many of us have ever encountered insurmountable problems trying to gain access to a copy of, to take some common examples, *Moby Dick* or *Bleak House*? If it is not available at the library, chances are that a local bookstore will have copies for sale. Granted, this is not always the case. But consider this also: what comfort does an electronic edition of *Moby Dick* provide to someone who does not own or have ready access to a computer, or who is not familiar with the interface commands and protocols required to retrieve *Moby Dick* from the files of Project Gutenberg? As difficult as it may be for us to grasp, even at this late date in human history, not everyone is computer literate. The world of computer technology is not yet the democratic realm we would like to think it is. And when Hart makes his claim that the creation of electronic texts "will undoubtedly become the greatest advance to human civilization and society since the invention of writing itself" (7), we have to draw back and decide for ourselves if there exists a factual basis for such a statement or if it is merely a self-serving proclamation from someone who may have lost touch with the real world.

Humans have been storing and reading words on a paper medium of one sort or another for hundreds of years, and, as the adage goes, "old habits are hard to break." We have seen that the driving forces behind transformations in communication technology include mundane factors such as the ease of use, compactness, portability. The book would appear to be the epitome of these features and the embodiment of many more.

> The advantages of printed books as a medium of information storage and exchange is that they are robust, they need zero power, several can be open at once, they have been around for 550 years, all literate people know how to use them, and they are readable in strong sunlight... (Rawlins)

Moreover, in the printed book, the text can be enhanced by the use of diagrams, charts, graphs, drawings, and photographs, and the subject matter can be indexed for easy and immediate access. Some would argue that today, with the availability of internet browsing software and other text-encoding systems, the electronic text offers all of this, as well as sound and moving pictures. Still, how could anyone prefer electronic text to the printed book, bound and encased on our shelves, an object to admire and refer to for the rest of our lives?

In fact, the electronic text offers a tangible advantage over the printed text, one that is described quite succinctly by Tom Maddox: "We might say that the electronic text is smarter than the printed text… [I]t contains information about itself that a printed text contains only when it has been thoroughly analyzed" (Maddox).

My question at the beginning of this section was "What can you do with an electronic version of Shakespeare's *Sonnets* that you cannot do with a print version?" The answer toward which I have been progressing is that the electronic version readily lends itself to textual and linguistic analysis; has, in fact, already *been* analyzed by virtue of its being rendered into electronic form. The electronic text is, in effect, a concordance to itself. The task of the scholar is to interpret an analysis that has already been performed, or, in other words, to learn to ask the text the right questions about itself. Maddox may be expressing the idea metaphorically, but to say that one is "smarter" than the other is simply to point out that electronic text can provide answers to questions about its structure and vocabulary while printed text remains mute. To the ordinary reader who wishes simply to settle in for a good read on a rainy afternoon, this answer may come as somewhat of a disappointment. But this feature actually represents a significant step forward in the burgeoning field of linguistics, a discipline in which the text itself is rigorously scrutinized in order to gain insight into its meaning and structure—and also in the field of literary studies, in which texts are compared and interpreted in light of any number of cultural, social, and historical perspectives. The gain for the student of literature is immense because if the text is available in electronic form the task of minutely examining each line, each page, for relevant passages need not be a part of the scholarly ordeal. Instead, a simple keyword search will identify passages that contain specified words or phrases. In the electronic text, every word and every phrase is immediately accessible. This is its one indisputable, qualitative advantage over the printed text.

As readers, we turn to the printed text automatically, almost without thinking. We prefer words on paper because that is what we are accustomed to, even though, as Tom Maddox argues, "the page and its structures, [though] efficient and convenient…have no more essential validity for reading than the tablet or the scroll, technologies of writing they superseded." The computer screen as both a reading and a writing space will doubtless become more prevalent in years to come, but whether it will actually supersede the paper medium remains a matter of some debate. I have no intention at this point of entering that discussion. However, I will provide a couple of quotations that exhibit the range of opinion currently circulating with regard to this topic.

> Paper will be with us for decades to come because of the hundreds of years of technological development behind simple, cheap, light, detachable pieces of paper, and the complementary use of hand and eye to arrange, read, or write them. (Rawlins)

> The book has lost its privilege. For those who camped in its shadows, for the culturally

homeless, this is not necessarily a bad thing. No less than the sitcom or the Nintendo cartridge, the book too is merely a fleeting, momentarily marketable, physical instantiation of the network. And the network, unlike the tower, is ours to inhabit. (Joyce "Notes Toward..." par. 5)

Electronic Communication and Networking

In the previous section we looked, albeit in a rather cursory fashion, at the issue of rendering standard works of literature into electronic form, pointing out some advantages of e-text and of print as mediums of communication. The works that are targeted by Project Gutenberg and other text conversion projects are normally works that have passed into the public domain and for which copyright is therefore not an issue. In cases such as this, the fact that countless electronic copies can be generated from a single source file does not cause anyone much concern. *Moby Dick* remains *Moby Dick* whether it has been copied once or a million times. The integrity of the text is not violated by duplication. Everyone will recognize it for what it is.

Combining e-text or electronic writing with electronic networking capabilities raises some other issues, ones of interest to the creative writer working today who uses the Internet and who may be considering electronic publication as a means of dissemination. My discussion of electronic communication and networking issues will of necessity be limited to matters having to do with the concept of authorship. On the other hand, networking is not a topic that can be dispensed with simply, and it will continue to arise within a number of varying contexts throughout the remainder of this volume.

With the appearance of articles in popular newsmagazines—first in *Time* (6 Dec . 1993), and then in *Newsweek* (16 May 1994)—the impact of electronic communications and networking systems, principally the Internet, became an object for public discussion. Tending to be glib in tone and superficial in content, these articles manage to create an impression of a global computer network crowded with 20 million or more users who have dialled in for trivial reasons such as enhancing their personal status or weather watching. They portray the Internet as "hip" and imply that if you are not "wired" you are hopelessly behind the times.

> Suddenly the Internet is the place to be. American college students are queuing up outside computing centers to get online. Executives are ordering new business cards that show off their Internet addresses. Millions of people around the world are logging on to tap into libraries, call up satellite weather photos, download free computer programs, and participate in discussion groups with everyone from lawyers to physicists to sadomasochists. (Elmer-Dewitt 44)

What the Internet may actually represent is a global classroom or workshop in which everyone who participates is simultaneously a teacher and a student. This is pure speculation because everyone's experience of the Net is different and people have different reasons for being there. However, there appears to be ample evidence to suggest that the interest of participants in the Net is sustained by what they can discover that is new, that is unfamiliar, or that is unusual; people communicate with one another on the Net because they are interested in what others have to say. This new application of electronic communication technology is nothing like television, where information flows in one direction only and before which people sit transfixed, passive recipients of sound and image; or the telephone with its one-to-one structure and its total reliance on voice. Instead, the Net demands a continuous exchange of information, requires its members to participate, to be interactive, to give of themselves as much as they receive from others. And what they mostly exchange is electronic text.

One of the long-standing features of the Internet is that its electronic mail messaging system divides participants into subject-oriented discussion groups, called listservs, in which each member is unequivocally identified as an individual with an interest in the topic specific to that list. Once you join a discussion list you receive copies of all e-mail postings sent to the group as a whole (unless you specify otherwise). The exchange process begins when someone returns a response to a general posting to the entire membership, thus initiating a series of e-text communications that anyone on the list is entitled to respond to, read, quote, copy, or ignore as they wish.

These exchanges can occur almost instantaneously. The potential exists for replies to an original posting to be received in a matter of seconds. This may seem like a description of a simple telephone voice transaction in which people exchange observations and respond to one another instantly. However, there are two features of e-mail communication—other than that it relies not on voice but on text—that set it apart from other forms of communication, verbal, visual, and textual.

First of all, in a great many cases, persons exchanging messages on the Net will know nothing about each other except a name and possibly the city or town, perhaps the organization, from which the messages originate. For some mysterious reason, this fact does not stand as an obstruction to communication; inhibitions that are manifest in the day-to-day world of human communication seem to evaporate on the Net. People who are total strangers will assume an unguarded intimacy—a camaraderie born of collective purpose and attitude—when communicating merely by virtue of sharing membership in a discussion group. Whether the dialogue is friendly or combative, the tendency on the Net is to open oneself up, to hold little or nothing back, to express oneself fully and without reserve.

The second feature that sets e-mail communication apart from other forms of informational interaction derives from the first. This is the "virtual" anonymity that characterizes almost all exchanges on the Net. When reading a posting on the computer screen, it is likely that we know nothing of the person who composed it other than a name. However, with repeated postings, the tone of a specific individual's messages becomes familiar. We come to recognize a person's voice, his or her distinctive vocabulary, choice of constructions, irregular or idiosyncratic usages. We begin to characterize people according to the words they use and how they choose to express themselves: "He is shy, pedantic, and ponderous," "She is vivacious and brash." Members of the Internet community become virtually identified with the words they use. As authors, they are linked to and inseparable from the texts they generate. On the Net, the text is more than just the author's voice; the text *is* the author, and the author *is* the text. This is an important factor to remember when we consider that much of postmodern critical theory has sought ways to break down links between author and text, claiming, in fact, that the text lives and breathes independently of the author's influence and that for all intents and purposes the author is dead.

However, as with most things in life, a paradox lurks at the heart of this view of Internet communication. Once an author dispatches a message into what is commonly called "cyberspace," all control over that communication is in effect relinquished. As authors, we have no way of knowing who, if anyone, will eventually read our words, what uses they may be put to, or who else, for that matter, may presume to claim authorship. We can attach our names to our compositions, but this is where the similarities with conventional (paper-based) forms of communication end. Electronic text is by its very nature malleable, fluid, unstable. Once a text has been captured at the local level it can be modified in any number of ways, and this is true of electronic text in general. Where electronic communications are concerned, releasing texts that we have composed into cyberspace is an act of either complete and utter folly, or else of the highest form of generosity. Either way you look at it, the author can be removed from the text quite easily. In a very literal sense, the text can be granted a life completely free of the author's influence. Whether this is a good thing or not depends upon your point of view. But it does open a debate into which many theorists have willingly rushed, one that calls into question the traditional authority of the author over the text, a concept that has descended to us nearly intact from the eighteenth century.

> When written words are stored as electronic bits in memory, they are not objects to be owned. When authors are incarnated as electronic texts that can be erased, annotated, downloaded, linked, and redistributed, they are "textualized"; at that point their identities merge into a communal hypertext or discussion thread. (Sewell)

I will be discussing these issues in greater detail in a later chapter. Suffice it to say at this point that the precise nature of the relationship between the author and the text in cyberspace is yet to be defined.

Despite the apparent dangers that await the author in cyberspace, the very real fact remains that the Internet provides a natural and congenial home for the creative writer. I can make such a statement boldly and without qualification because of my personal experience as a member of a discussion group called CREWRT-L, Creative Writing in Education for Teachers and Students.

In the words of John Oughton, forwarded by Eric Crump, the members of CREWRT-L include "teachers, students, poets, novelists, essayists, critics, short-story writers, Baha'ais, Episcopalians, Texans, Canadians, parents, gays, straights, weather-watchers, administration-denouncers, libs, cons, and magnificently in-betweenies." As one can see, the membership is eclectic and geographically wide-ranging. Members come to creative writing from a variety of backgrounds, but the majority are either academics or university students. The list is populated by individuals who represent a broad range of experience within the discipline of creative writing, from established authors with several books to their credit to the novice who is just beginning to develop a voice and overcome the initial fears of self-expression. However, once the connection has been made, all are treated as equals within the egalitarian realm of cyberspace.

As far as the matter of discussion is concerned, Oughton claims that the subject "is whatever we want it to be by consensus and force of eloquence. We do sometimes discuss creative writing pedagogy and practice, literary theory, contests, publications, and famous writers" (Crump). In fact, discussions range far and wide, from topics of serious literary concern to matters of the day.

Theories abound with regard to the forces that impel certain individuals and not others to seek expression through poetry and creative prose, psychological hypotheses that strive to identify the primal urge that ultimately causes pen to make contact with paper. My own belief is that each person's reasons for choosing to write creatively are different, and each of us derives benefits from the experience that are unique to ourselves. I will, however, venture one generalization, and that is that within the psyche of the creative writer there resides a volatile mix of ego and self-doubt, that the experience of the creative writer is one of dazzling achievement and, equally, one of abject failure. To survive in any creative endeavour, an artist needs support and encouragement: psychic or spiritual nourishment of one sort or another. I suppose it is possible for a writer to provide this for him- or herself and in this way become self-sustaining. But I think this is very rare. In most cases writers find it salutary to have some means of expressing the joys and the frustrations that are an essential part of the craft. It is the contention of W. Scott Olsen that the Internet furnishes just such an outlet by providing writers, who may very well be separated by vast physical distances, with a ready channel through which to make contact and exchange their messages of grief and exultation.

> [As] writers gain experience and authority and trust in their own visions, the location of their sustenance changes from external stories of people engaged in similar writing/ publishing struggles to internal stories of people engaged in moral/ethical/situational struggles that reflect and recreate the author's own sensibility as a member of [a] particular culture. In other words, all writers are sustained by a mythic sense of community. (Olsen)

Creative writers do not work in isolation. In order to begin writing at all, an individual must envision a personal locus on the literary continuum from pre-history to the present day. Writers must also discover for themselves a haven within a community of persons whose aspirations are similar. Sending a general message to CREWRT-L and receiving in short order a number of replies expressing a commonality of purpose is a heartening experience. It also reminds us of the profoundly human element that the realm of the electronic messaging system can sometimes mask.

> I have not met most of the people I can claim as electronic or virtual friends. Yet these people have become important to me. The community we share is not one of place but one of temperament, of habit, of ambition and desire, of love and anger. The Internet creates, I think for the first time in human history, a mythic community into which I can gain real-time access. (Olsen)

Olsen's "mythic community" is not a product of an overactive imagination. It is a psychic region within the author's mind that is evoked each time data bits travelling over the lines of the network converge at the local site and are displayed across the screen as text. The text in turn conveys the authorial presence behind it, tells of the thought and energy that were expended in the act of creating it. The recipient of many messages senses the presence of many writers, and thus the community is born.

Electronic Publication

What does publication mean to writers? For many it represents the ultimate endorsement of themselves as artists or scholars. They have an idea, they explore it, refine it, and through the combined effort of reason and an aesthetic sensibility, transform it into a work of prose or poetry. Revision comes next, a lengthy process. Eventually the work must be submitted to a publisher, if only because many writers will continue to revise endlessly, and often aimlessly, if they refrain from placing the results of their efforts into someone else's hands for evaluation. The acceptance is both thrilling and gratifying, first of all because most artists lack the objective capacity to judge the value of their own work, and secondly, because it means that an utter stranger who has no connection to the author other than through the text has been convinced the work is of sufficient merit to justify printing and distributing hundreds, perhaps thousands, of copies. Implicit in the offer of publication is the presumption that people will derive pleasure and maybe even edification from the act of reading the author's text.

Apart from the simple fact that artists will be encouraged by this, or indeed any, positive feedback, there is the added distinction for the writer of being thereafter manifest in the text. Publication means that there exists a great many objects bearing the name and perhaps the image of the author, but over which the author can exert no control other than that provided by copyright law. People are free to draw inferences concerning the author from the work. In fact, the author can write more works of quite a different nature, the author can quit writing altogether, or die, or perhaps even repudiate the work. However, the initial work will continue to exist and be there for others to read and interpret and from which to draw conclusions. Once publication has occurred, the author is inextricably bound to the text. Nothing can change this.

Can this experience be transferred to the electronic environment? What, if anything, does electronic publication mean?

I wish to make clear precisely what I am referring to when I speak of "electronic publication." I intend to limit my discussion to those works of a creative or scholarly nature—stories, poems, novels, critical articles, personal communications—that are available over the Internet. Of necessity, I will not be considering bibliographic databases that appear as remote data files or as CD-ROMs, and, in fact, will not be including CD-ROM in my discussion at all. I am also compelled to omit from my discussion editions of canonical works that are appearing with increasing frequency these days on floppy disk. I will instead concentrate on the Internet because it is within this largely ungovernable and tumultuous communications network that electronic publication is becoming a volatile and contentious issue. Electronic journals are proliferating at a rate that would likely astound those who made forecasts in this area only a few years ago. Text files of various kinds are accessible at countless Internet sites, stored on local mainframes and available via anonymous File Transfer Protocol (FTP), over the Gopher or the World Wide Web (WWW). Writers are quickly gaining the skills and expertise needed to distribute their own works across the globe, if that's what they want to do. And this raises the question that if a work is widely available, does it somehow gain a prestige or validity greater than another similar work that resides only in the form of a text file on the hard drive of its author's personal computer? How does this relate to our traditional concept of "publication"?

To be a creative writer with a goal of seeing one's work in print requires a great deal of patience as well as tenacity, a belief in oneself, and a willingness to persist against the odds. It is common for the author of a work of poetry or creative prose to wait anywhere from two months to a year to hear from the editor of a journal once a piece has been submitted. Where articles submitted to academic journals are concerned, the wait can be even longer because of the complexities of a peer review process that requires several readers to arrive at a consensus regarding the merits of a paper. Though hardly desirable, these delays are excused by writers as the price to be paid for knowing their work is being considered seriously for publication, which, if it occurs, means they have been accepted into a national cultural or literary heritage and that their voice will be heard and can make a difference. Of course, the number of people who may actually read the work after it has been published can be affected by many factors. Some, such as the relevance of the topic or the appeal of the characters or storyline in a piece of fiction, the author can control. Others, perhaps the quality and availability of the journal, which may not receive wide distribution or may not be on the subscription lists of a great many libraries or individuals, are beyond the author's sphere of influence. The same can be said of publication in book form. If the book is not marketed aggressively or reviewed widely, the community of readers exposed to the author's message may be very small indeed.

This scenario illustrates a contradiction intrinsic to the mechanism of publication, one that hinges on the objectives of writers who actively seek widespread dissemination of their work.

By simply initiating a search for a publishing outlet, the writer is expressing a desire for least one of two things, and probably both: to see his or her work in the hands of as many readers as possible, and to receive legitimization as a writer by having the work accepted by peers in the literary community, in this instance the editors and readers labouring on behalf of literary and academic journals. There are not likely to be many other reasons for submitting works of fiction or poetry to journals; monetary remuneration is certainly not a realistic consideration. Writers who do not find the intangible rewards of publication sufficiently attractive are probably not sharing their work with a wide body of readers either.

What is there to stop writers from photocopying their work and distributing it indiscriminately on the street? Nothing, except maybe the suspicion that the work will not be regarded seriously by those into whose hands it happens to fall. Writers who take upon themselves the dual role of publisher and distributor are risking exactly this: that their work will thereafter be regarded as inconsequential by the very people whose approval they seek. The calibre of the work is not important. If the only voice espousing its merits is the writer's own, then it is unlikely that the work will receive serious critical attention, whether or not this attention is warranted.

The issue here is quality. The task of an editor of a literary or scholarly journal, or an editor at a publishing house, is to examine submissions, determine which of them are worthwhile, and then ensure that these are published and offered to an appropriate audience. There is a conspicuous element of blind trust involved in this process. Readers purchase books and journals because they trust editors to publish only that material which is worthy of their attention. Writers trust editors to be truthful and honest in their assessments of the work that crosses their desks and to accept only that work which attains a sufficient level of merit. If for any reason a perception evolves and spreads that the publishing standards of a journal are deteriorating, the credibility of both editor and journal is damaged, its reservoir of reputable contributors dries up, the quality of submissions declines, the journal loses its readership, the journal folds, the editor is out of a job.

All of this is by way of a preamble to the issues raised by the concept of "publication" on the Internet. Whether we like it or not—and opinion is very divided—technology now exists that makes it possible for anyone with the proper equipment to distribute their work as widely as they please using electronic means. There is an almost limitless range of alternatives, from sending a poem, story, or essay to a single other Net user through direct electronic mail, to loading the text file on a local mainframe and making it available to everyone through the Gopher and anonymous FTP, to encoding the text file with Hypertext Markup Language (HTML) commands and posting it on the WWW. Much of the literature on the topic of electronic publication dwells on electronic scholarly journals. But the discussion can be applied with equal appropriateness to the purely creative realm as well, where proponents of quality stand in opposition to advocates of Net openness.

One of the issues often raised with regard to publication on the Internet is the ambiguous nature of the enterprise. As Charles Bailey observes, "it is not always easy to tell where informal conference activity ends and formal electronic publication begins" ("Electronic (Online) Publishing in Action" 28). Indeed, if I were to upload a short story complete with copyright declaration from my PC to the local mainframe and from there forward it to everyone on the CREWRT-L mailing list, would this mean that the story had been "published"? In a sense, I have created three to four hundred copies of my story and placed it in a situation where it is likely to be perused by some, if not all, of a potential readership. Further, my action has resulted in the existence of several hundred autonomous "objects" that have my name attached to them but over which I can exert no control. The recipients of my story are free to read, delete, download, or print it as they choose. They can even erase my name from the by-line and copyright note and claim the work as their own, if they are so inclined. The fluid nature of electronic writing makes all of these scenarios possible, if not desirable. But even though my work has been widely distributed and possibly read by many people, can I reasonably claim that it has been "published"?

The answer is, of course, that I cannot. What I have done is no different than if I had made three hundred copies of my story and mailed it to three hundred of my friends. The story has not passed through an editorial or peer-review process, the step that many regard as the crucial factor distinguishing publication from simple distribution.

Much of the dialogue concerning this topic centres around the notion that electronic text is intrinsically fluid and therefore ephemeral, while printed text is material and therefore permanent. The trouble with the debate as it appears in the literature is that the majority of articles adopt a defensive or offensive stance as they argue the merits of one format in an attempt to discredit the other. While it is true that both formats can boast advantages while conceding certain disadvantages, I think the discussion would be better served by examining the issues and leaving the reader to make up his or her own mind.

To many humanities scholars,

> Electronic journals are viewed as impermanent, less satisfying to read, and it is feared their contents will change as the journals are disseminated. Therefore, these journals may be suitable for reflecting what is transient in scholarship; what is permanent and authoritative should be preserved in print. (Harrison, Stephen, and Winter 29)

The above noted concern is one that is very real, one that persists in the minds of readers, and one that may ultimately prevent the presentation of digital texts on the Internet from achieving anything more than the status of an interim step in the lengthy process leading to preservation in print form. By its very nature electronic text—the ASCII text file that can be printed or downloaded straight off the Net—has about it a generic appearance, a tedious sameness that cannot even begin to challenge the professionally printed text for simple aesthetic appeal. In the majority of cases, what appears on the screen has no distinguishing characteristics, nothing of an individual stamp to set it apart from thousands of other electronic texts. William Arms notes that systems that present electronic text

> are no threat to the printed document. All that can be displayed is unformatted text, usually in a fixed spaced font, without diagrams, mathematics, or the graphic quality that makes a well-designed document. When these defects are added to the inherent defects of a computer screen—poor contrast and low resolution—it is hardly surprising that many people are convinced that scholars will never be willing to read from a screen. (Arms 165)

Apart from the purely physical limitations imposed on those who endeavour to read lengthy documents on the computer screen, there is as well a certain ambiguity inherent in the perception—or misperception—that what they are reading is actually a publication of some sort, by which I mean a document that has been read, evaluated, and approved for distribution by someone other than the author. How is the reader to know for sure if the document has passed through any sort of review process?

The fact is that there are now a great many reputable electronic journals accessible on the Net—*The Public Access Computer Systems Review, Postmodern Culture, Intertext, The Gutter Voice,* to name but a few—the editors of which apply the same rigorous standards of professionalism to their publications as do the editors of print journals. There is a difference, however.

> Electronic learned journals which respect current norms work in just the same way as a conventional journal; the time between the receipt of the corrected manuscript and its setting in definitive form is about the same: a matter of weeks. But once this point is reached the article can be put immediately at the disposal of researchers, for an electronic journal is not limited, by costs, to the publication of only a few hundred pages a year. (Guédon 4)

In exchange, then, for perceived insubstantiality, the e-journal provides instantaneous access, which means that new ideas, poetry, and fiction can be discussed while they are still fresh and germane rather than languishing in editorial offices for the interminable waiting period that precedes the appearance in print form. Ann Okerson, expanding on this view of electronic publication, points out that

> the idea is sprouted precisely when it is ready, critiqued via the "Net" and put out immediately for wide examination or "open peer commentary." Ideas that might have been stillborn in paper come alive as other scholars respond with alacrity and collaborate to improve knowledge systems. (9)

Will the speed of delivery be enough to convince humanities scholars to publish their work in electronic form? As yet there is no clear answer. However, Okerson hints at yet another feature of electronic publication that may prove enticing and which emerges directly from its immediate accessibility. This is the potential for interactive and collaborative efforts within the electronic community of scholars to improve and build upon ideas as they appear. This feature is as well of interest to creative writers who distribute early drafts of their work on discussion lists such as CREWRT-L and solicit feedback and suggestions. From here we can make a conceptual leap to a different view of writing altogether and ask if electronic publication will "alter or do away with our very idea of the finished work, the authoritative text, the final product?" (Amiran, Orr, and Unsworth 36). Amiran, Orr, and Unsworth further suggest that "the dynamic nature of e-texts allows us to recognize contradiction, change and difference as the standard features of complex thinking, rather than fearing them as inimical to thought" (36).

We can see why consensus is so difficult to achieve when the very same ephemerality and mutability that Harrison, Stephen, and Winter view with alarm is regarded by Amiran, Orr, and Unsworth as an advantage.

Another vocal and active proponent of electronic publication, Stevan Harnad, sees the potential for the ceaseless evolution of ideas on the Net as a momentous and positive step in the history of scholarly inquiry. Much of his writing applauds the possibilities being opened up by the new technology and as well poses a direct challenge to the entire concept of the static, paper-bound publication. He regards paper publication as a natural outgrowth of the technology that was available at the time. However, with the emergence of electronic writing systems, there is now no excuse for us to remain bound by the constraints imposed by print or to assume that the final form of any idea will be its internment on the printed page.

> Electronic publication is not just a more efficient implementation of paper publishing; it offers the possibility of a phase transition in the form (and hence also the content) of scholarly writing. Not only are the boundaries between "informal" and "formal" literature blurred, but scholarly inquiry has always been a continuum, from the inchoate birth of new ideas and findings to their (in principle) endless evolution as inquiry carries on. (Harnad, "Interactive Publication" 59)

In his writings, Harnad has envisioned for us the possibility of harnessing the advantages of the print publication—in particular, the process of peer-review—within the electronic medium, where scholarly collaboration is not only probable, but inevitable, and founded the e-journal *Psycholoquy* based on this principle. He calls this interactive capability in the electronic realm "Scholarly Skywriting," and further states, "this is what I predict will prove to be the invaluable new communicative possibility the Net offers to scholars, the one that paper could never hope to implement" (Harnad, "Scholarly Skywriting" 13).

I have no intention of attempting to refute Harnad's prophecies, which for all I know many prove to be accurate, and only wish to point out the need to proceed with caution, to continually test our assumptions, and to avoid being seduced by rhetoric. Though they are multiplying with great speed, electronic journals are still in their infancy, and it is by no means clear if they will ever be universally adopted as the successor to their paper progenitor. As I noted earlier, there are a great many e-journals currently available that strive for the same degree of scholarly credibility and "prestige" as their paper counterparts. However, there are also a number of electronic publications, as there are print publications, that are not rigorous about standards, and there are as well numerous local sites that are making unrefereed papers available in pre-print form. Frank Quinn cautions against the unquestioning acceptance of electronic publications, arguing that we should not allow ourselves to be bullied into regarding everything that emanates from over the wire as authoritative and conclusive, even if the alternative is to be labelled as a technophobe. It is much more important, he says, to ensure the integrity of the literature by demanding that high quality remains the ultimate standard by which any writing must be measured in order to achieve publication.

> In many areas there are already electronic preprint databases through which papers can be immediately circulated world-wide. They sometimes hit the wires a few seconds after the final keystrokes, and needless to say often not in final form. If the work is reviewed

and corrected before it is frozen into the literature, then the additional exposure is a good thing. But there are pressures to regard this instantaneous circulation as publication. Information can be transmitted instantly, so authors want credit instantly. They want to stay in the flow of ideas rather than take the time to nail the last one down firmly. (Quinn, "Roadkill")

Quinn calls upon everyone—readers, editors, writers—to make "a strong distinction between preprints and material which has been officially accepted into the literature, either paper or electronic" (Quinn, "Roadkill"). By maintaining this distinction, any dangers to the literature of the sciences, humanities, and the social sciences—danger in the form of degradation of quality—will be for the moment averted.

Throughout this discussion I have been referring in general terms to the issue of providing access to scholarly papers over the Internet. And though the focus of this inquiry is the humanities, the concerns I have raised are likely to be similar for all researchers and academics considering Internet publication regardless of subject interest or field of specialization.

Is the issue the same for writers of creative literary works? It is true that timeliness is not usually a vital consideration for fiction or poetry, works that, if they are any good, should endure throughout time. But like other artists, creative writers like to see their work placed before an audience in a timely fashion, and the Internet offers them the opportunity to distribute their writing immediately upon completion. But is this something we should all begin taking advantage of today? Again, it is a matter for the individual writer to decide. Under normal conditions, however, a work of creative literature passes through a period of gestation in the author's mind before being committed either to paper or the computer screen. During the process of composition, works of this nature customarily undergo profound transformations and often become something quite different from what the author originally envisioned. Early drafts of novels and stories can reveal how ideas evolve and merge with other ideas, how voice develops and character issues forth from narrative and narrative from character. All this is to say that a novel, story, or poem is not necessarily finished just because it has been granted the physical tangibility required for others to be able to read it. Creative writers often set works aside after they have been written and then return to them months, or even years, later with a new approach and a fresh perspective. Many writers do not want readers interfering in this process. Feedback is helpful to a point, but too much can be suffocating. And even when an author believes a work is finished and ready for an audience, sometimes the best thing that can occur is a lengthy submission process or a delay prior to publication. Having the work returned again and again forces the writer to consider changes that may not earlier have come to mind. Any serious creative writer will welcome the opportunity to make revisions and improve a work before it goes before an audience.

But again, this is for the individual to decide. There are probably many works of fiction and poetry that, because of an editor's misjudgment, have been prematurely made available in print form, and this is regrettable. However, the instant and widespread exposure offered by the Internet's powerful communication capabilities constitute a serious enticement to writers who want to get their work out there. For some writers there is no doubt a real temptation to bypass the review process altogether and post the work on the Net, finished or not.

Unquestionably opinions on this matter will vary, but it seems reasonable to expect responsible writers doing serious work to seek out reputable e-journals—and there is a growing number that include evaluation and review as part of the editorial process—and to make their submissions to these. The rewards of distributing one's own work on the Net are dubious at best, unless of course the only goal is to get it into as many hands as possible.

There is no telling where the technology will take us next. Standardized markup languages such as HTML, the ready availability of WWW browsers such as Netscape and Mosaic, and the relatively inexpensive equipment and connections needed to access the Internet, have made it theoretically possible for anyone connected to the Internet to publish their own e-journal. Who can say at this point whether or not such a development is desirable? However, my own feeling with regard to serious and reputable e-journals is that external pressures—primarily economic—will come to bear upon whether or not they grow into a forceful presence on the global publication scene. As the ecological downturn continues paper may become a scarce and prohibitively expensive commodity, forcing publishers to seek alternatives. On the other hand, paper may remain plentiful and cheap, and publishers of print journals may respond to the challenges facing them by lowering prices, abbreviating the publication process, and introducing elements of interactivity in imitation of e-journals. With something as fluid and volatile as electronic publication forecasts are of limited use. The technology as we know it today could very well be obsolete tomorrow. However, as responsible users of this technology, we should do all we can to ensure that we are in a position to benefit from any advantages that may accrue.

Hypertext

Stated quite simply, hypertext is "nonsequential writing" (Landow, *Hypertext* 4). More elaborately, it is "an information technology consisting of individual blocks of text, or lexias, and the electronic links that join them" (Landow, "What's a Critic to Do?" 1). Or, to speak pragmatically, it is a method of textual programming that allows for an almost unlimited number of directional permutations and therefore an almost unlimited number of readings or interpretations. The reader of a hypertext is placed by the author in the position of constructing a personal version of the text, one that may in fact be unique and which quite possibly may never be duplicated. The reader makes choices of direction, decides how the story will unfold, passes over one narrative thread in favour of another. In theory, if not in practise, this process can continue forever because, unlike conventional narratives, hypertexts do not draw inexorably toward a conclusion. Rather, hypertexts invite the reader into a web of possibilities, continually offering choice upon choice, renewing themselves at every turn. The author of a hypertext vanishes as the reader takes control and begins weaving a private story thread. Where hypertext is concerned, the reader appears to represent the ultimate authority.

Attempts to define hypertext abound, but I believe the above statement provides a fair assessment and gives a reasonable impression of its capabilities. The abiding principle of hypertext resides in the element of choice, a feature that turns traditional narrative forms with their undeviating linearity on their collective ear and empowers the reader to take the initiative and to forge new paths. In fact, the experience of hypertext is not so much one of reading as it is one of "navigation." And it is here that we begin to echo the claims of other writers who regard hypertext as a "place" or "space" distinct from the one which literature has occupied for hundreds of years: the printed page—or even the last twenty years: the computer screen.

Though new to many people, the concept of hypertext has actually been with us for several decades (Ted Nelson coined the term in the 1960s to describe a method of nonlinear writing), but it is only in recent years that the technology has enabled programmers and authors to actively explore the capabilities of such systems. The Internet itself is in fact a huge unruly hypertextual structure to which browsers such as Mosaic and Netscape attempt to bring some order. Electronic encyclopedias and dictionaries are useful and more powerful than their printed precursors because of their hypertext capabilities. And electronic publishers such as Eastgate Systems have been making hypertext fictions commercially available for many years now.

As far back as 1963, however, when the Argentinean writer Julio Cortázar published his revolutionary novel *Rayuela*, translated as *Hopscotch* in 1966 by Gregory Rabassa, a form of limited hypertext became a reality. The novel comes complete with a "Table of Instructions" which reads in part:

> In its own way, this book consists of many books, but two books above all. The first can be read in a normal fashion and it ends with Chapter 56, at the close of which there are three garish little stars which stand for the words *The End*. Consequently, the reader may ignore what follows with a clean conscience.
>
> The second should be read by beginning with Chapter 73 and then following the sequence indicated at the end of each chapter. In case of confusion or forgetfulness, one need only consult the following list. (Cortázar [i])

At this point there follows a sequence of chapter numbers that to the casual observer appears completely random.

By granting us the power to make choices that can influence the flow of the narrative, Cortázar is engaging in hypertextuality. His novel draws us into a weblike structure that demands that we as readers involve ourselves in the storymaking process. It challenges our conventional aspiration as readers to discover within the text an ideal meaning or interpretation, and it subverts our expectations of linearity and closure. Admittedly, the book *does* come to an end, but we can always return to it and read the chapters in a different order, and thereby experience a somewhat different text.

Undoubtedly by doing all of this Cortázar abdicates certain of the author's responsibilities. But there is no question either that *Hopscotch* is a great work of literature, one that stands on its own apart from its hypertextual design. Indeed, the chapters can be read in numerical order and the hypertextuality of the novel safely ignored with no depreciation of the text as a work of art. It is obvious to anyone who has ever read *Hopscotch* that Cortázar's primary concern was with standard literary attributes such as complex characterization, rich imagery, atmospheric setting, and engaging incident. The hypertextual design, though it enhances the reading experience offered by this novel, is secondary.

Can this also be said of modern electronic hypertexts? Do these works successfully engage us as readers apart from their hypertextual structure, a feature that could be looked upon as little more than a clever literary gimmick masking the mediocrity of the text? Of course, there is no way to adequately answer this question without launching into a close inspection of these texts, something that is beyond the scope of the present undertaking. I wish, therefore, to simply examine hypertext in light of the current debate and to reflect upon any advantages that authors and readers can expect to gain from this technology.

> A hypertext is like a printed book that the author has attacked with a pair of scissors and cut into convenient verbal sizes. The difference is that the electronic hypertext does not simply dissolve into a disordered bundle of slips, as the printed book must. For the author also defines a scheme of electronic connections to indicate relationships among the slips. In fashioning a hypertext, a writer might begin with a passage of continuous prose and then add notes or glosses on important words in the passage....[T]he glosses themselves could contain glosses, leading the reader to further texts. A hypertextual network can extend indefinitely, as a printed text cannot. (Bolter 24)

We can see from this description how hypertext allows the reader to jump from one location within the text to another, exploring links and making connections, on a quest for further and still further information. And within the context of reference tools and research documents such as encyclopedias and dictionaries this radical restructuring is no problem and, in fact, makes perfect sense and can even represent a distinct advantage. Having entered the hypertextual structure, the reader's investigation of a topic is no longer hindered by physical impediments such as intervening pages, or the need to drop one volume and pick up another. Instead, the reader selects a link and follows it directly to the next piece of relevant text, which is displayed on the screen the instant the choice is made. With the author's physical arrangement of the information thus circumvented, the process of inquiry and learning appears to form a direct line from idea to understanding, an unobstructed journey in the pursuit of knowledge and information.

> Hypertext basically destroys the authority of the author to determine how readers should be introduced to a topic. From the readers' perspective, this is one of the great advantages of hypertext since it means that they are free to explore the information as they see fit. (Nielsen 171)

This is fine for small bites of information, such as the brief articles found in encyclopedias, but what does all this leaping about do to the narrative continuity of fiction and poetry? Obviously, it breaks it up—fragments it—fractures it. Narrative momentum is, if not destroyed, then seriously impaired. The act of reading as an endeavour to find out what happens next is forever altered.

"Hypertext has no necessary beginning and end, hence no unitary completeness; it will not allow us to finish—we are reading it or we have stopped reading it; we have never read it" (Maddox).

If the experience of the reader is so altered, can we assume that the experience of the author is altered as well? This would appear to be the case, simply because hypertext requires a radically altered way of thinking, one that does not view cause and effect as the building blocks of narrative. The causal relationship between events upon which much of conventional narrative depends has been subverted. In its place appear programmed links between words—hypertextual loops that propel us forward and backward within the text, or out of the text altogether. The author of a hypertext is not primarily concerned with consistency of characterization or unity of space, time, or style, or any of the formalities or conventions that have aided in the discussion of works of literature for hundreds of years. Instead, the author of a hypertextual work seeks to evoke a plurality of interesting experiences, at the very minimum one for each reader who encounters the text. Some may point out that this could be said of any work of literature whose author hopes that every reader derives something from the text that is personal and unique. However, the distinction between conventional narrative and hypertextual narrative is this: whereas conventional narrative can exist quite nicely even when many readers happen to derive similar meanings from the experience of reading it, hypertext exists only when many readers derive a multiplicity of experiences. If the hypertextual choices are not made, hypertext ceases to fulfil its function and cannot be said to exist.

> We find ourselves at the confluence of twentieth-century narrative arts and cognitive science as they approach an age of machine-based art [and] virtual realities....The new writing requires rather than encourages multiple readings. It not only enacts these readings, it does not exist without them. Multiple fictions accomplish what its [sic] progenitors could only aspire to, lacking a topographic medium, light speed, electronic grace, and the willing intervention of the reader. (Joyce, "Notes Toward..." par. 45)

Though I admire his eloquence and agree with much of what he says, I would take issue with Joyce's assertion that hypertext represents the culmination of what writers have been aspiring to for centuries. It may be true that hypertext evokes a myriad of readings, but it does this only through the programmed intervention of the author, from which the reader cannot escape without undermining the hypertextual experience. Conventional narrative evokes multiple readings through devices such as linguistic shading and moral ambiguity. If the writing is sufficiently subtle and ingenious, interpretation will vary from reader to reader and all interpretations will contain elements of truth and of error. Conventional narrative demands that the reader take the lead and use what the author has provided to arrive at a conclusion, one that derives from a subjective response to the text and which may not even have been anticipated by the author. In hypertext, the reader may be making choices at every turn but is nonetheless following a trail of electronic cues provided by the author. Hypertext beguiles its readers with a false sense of autonomy, because no matter where their choices steer the narrative—no matter what dark corners they may swerve around or serpentine paths down which they may venture—they cannot take the story anywhere that the author has not already been.

There remains much to be said about hypertext, both as a learning tool and as a narrative device. New books are appearing all the time. Regardless of how we feel about the new technologies, the topography of the text *is* changing. And this will ultimately affect the way we approach and think about text. Perhaps the most profound challenge presented by today's hypertexts is directed toward our linear mode of reading and of using language in general. For thousands of years humans have accepted linearity as a standard feature of all communication. Idea follows idea in a logical sequence or progression, building toward a concluding argument or proof. In narrative fiction, event follows event. The reader recalls the one when reading about the next. Conventional literary fiction abounds with devices—characterization, symbol, foreshadowing—that depend for their effectiveness upon adherence to linear structure. Even modern poetry, for all its appearance of spontaneity on the page, depends upon a linear organization to articulate its meaning. Obviously we are not going to dispense with linear discourse tomorrow. But, as McKnight, Dillon, and Richardson point out, "The arrival of hypertext with its non-linear, modular, semantic structure has encouraged many proponents to claim that this new medium can loosen constraints on the way ideas are presented, accessed and even conceived" (McKnight, Dillon, and Richardson 16).

Can any serious attempt to discuss a new medium of communication be made within a system that does not allow features of that new medium to be incorporated? I'll leave this question without an answer and merely point out that to my knowledge there is yet to be published a hypertextual discussion of hypertext. Many of us who know what hypertext is and does are still waiting to experience it in the lengthy concentrated doses that would enable us to fully comprehend and appreciate its capabilities. A fundamental irony will persist until such time that hypertext becomes a commonplace object and transcends its current status as an electronic novelty or toy. As George Landow notes, "Until the time that computer technology...develops to the point that hypertext becomes a major, even if not yet dominant, medium, writers will continue to produce print-based discussions of it" (Landow, "What's a Critic to Do?" 35-6). And, as McKnight, Dillon, and Richardson add,

> At the most basic level, there is a need for both authors and readers to gain experience of hypertext. Readers of paper documents have a wealth of experience and document types

[and] have developed a variety of reading strategies and manipulation techniques. It will require use of hypertext over some time before users begin to develop the equivalent skills in hypertext. (137)

Despite the preceding argument, and Cortázar's *Hopscotch* notwithstanding, the fact remains that hypertext systems represent a departure from traditional print-based modes of textual presentation. This is especially true of hypertext fiction. As the reader makes the choices necessary to drive the story forward, a new cognitive space or field opens up which is composed of autonomous narrative sections. These fragments present themselves to the reader's mind as meaningful subdivisions of a larger whole, which the reader will never experience. "Meaning" emerges as links are followed, connections are made, and text is read and digested. Readers discover meaning because that is what they are looking for, the search for meaning is inherent in how their minds operate, even within an unfamiliar storyscape. However, the definitive "meaning" of any hypertext fiction is always going to be elusive, for the simple reason that the text in its entirety is inaccessible. The most any reader can hope for is a personal vision that may or may not include elements of a more comprehensive "meaning." As Michael Joyce observes, "Within the mythic system of emerging order the reader's task is to make meaning by perceiving order in space" (*Of Two Minds* 190).

It is also useful to note that much of the meaning we derive from a work of fiction or poetry comes from a sense of having completed it, of having read every word. Closure is important to us because it signals the end of possibility. We know that the narrative itself cannot change further, even though our interpretation of it might. Hypertext, however, demands a revision of common notions of closure. We may never actually finish reading it, as Tom Maddox observes, but it is probably accurate to say that we commenced reading it knowing that at some point we would decline to follow further links and read no further, that we would exit from the system and switch the machine off. Pulling the plug *does* constitute an ending of sorts, but hardly the inevitable ending of a novel or poem in which we finally reach the last page, the last line, the last word. It is an ending only in the sense that any action that cannot be continued forever has an ending implicit within the very act of doing it. We as human beings come to an end, we anticipate an end to everything. As J. Yellowlees Douglas observes, "Even though in interactive narratives, we as readers never encounter anything quite so definitive as the words 'The End,' or the last page of a story or novel, our experience of the text is not only guided but enabled by our sense of the 'ending' awaiting us" (185). Like many other aspects of the hypertextual experience, the "end" is dictated by the reader, which helps make it possible for the reader to embark upon that experience in the first place.

And what of literary criticism? Is it possible to discuss works of fiction or poetry when each reader's experience is different from all others? It could be argued that this is in fact the case for all fiction and poetry, both printed and electronic; that each reader comes away from the text with something unique, moved in a manner that is distinct from all other readers. But what happens when the actual words and the order in which they are encountered differs from reader to reader, when a specific reading of the text cannot be duplicated by subsequent readers? If this were the case, how could one person ever hope to write about or lecture on a hypertext authoritatively, to take most or even some possible interpretations into account? George Landow admits that "Large hypertexts and cybertexts simply offer too many lexias for critics ever to read. Quantity removes mastery and authority, for one can only sample, not master, a text" (Landow, "What's a Critic to Do?" 34-5). And further along: "in the nonreproducible text, critics find themselves in a situation analogous to the pre-print world, in which scribal drift insured that one could never be sure that another reader had read precisely the same text" (Landow, "What's a Critic to Do?" 35).

It is possible, then, that we are making a serious error to judge, or even to discuss, hypertexts while notions of conventional narrative structures continue to prevail and guide that discussion. We must approach hypertext with a new set of expectations, for the experience promises something other than that to which we are accustomed.

Sven Birkerts declares that "We do not know yet whether hypertext will ever be accepted by a mass readership as something more than a sophisticated Nintendo game played with language" (164). And therein lies the dilemma for theorists, such as myself, who presume to discuss a technology whose potential has hardly even been grasped let alone realized. Prophecies are fragile at the best of times, technological prophesies even more so.

What role will hypertext play in our lives? I do not feel that it will displace the conventional linear narrative as the storytelling medium of choice anytime soon. That it has value as a means of conveying information and supporting research is not under dispute. It has been demonstrated to be of use as a feature of encyclopedic and other reference works, and also as a method of presenting canonical texts that require heavy glossing and which benefit from having links drawn from one concept to a related one. But, as even some enthusiasts admit, without widespread acceptance and availability, as a method of storytelling it is likely to remain little more than a digital curiosity, despite its admittedly revolutionary structure and capabilities, for quite some time to come.

Or perhaps hypertext is merely telling us a different kind of story, one that many of us are not yet prepared or equipped to hear. A story with a fluid structure, with no beginning and no conclusion, a story that can move either forward or backward but which moves nowhere until we tell it where to go. It will take some adjustment for us to appreciate this story. As human beings, we can look in only one direction at a time. It is not our natural inclination to bounce through a disjointed narrative that may never end. That is not the way life is lived. In our search for meaning we surely look for connections, but for now many of us prefer to follow a real, as opposed to a virtual, path to a satisfying resolution.

> As readers, most of us have a model of a text, and that model demands that there be ultimately one story...that even if we cannot immediately grasp [it], could be grasped by some all-seeing observer—we believe in a Newtonian cosmos of fiction, in other words, not an Einsteinian or, more radically, [a] quantum mechanical one. (Maddox)

3

The Creative Process

In answering the question, How are poems made? my instinctive answer is a flat 'I don't know.' It makes not the slightest difference that the question as asked me refers solely to my own poems, for I know as little of how they are made as I do of any one else's. What I do know about them is only a millionth part of what there must be to know. I meet them where they touch consciousness, and that is already a considerable distance along the road of evolution.

Amy Lowell, "The Process of Making Poetry" from *The Creative Process* 109.

All writing is an attempt to represent ideas in symbolic form. Writers deal exclusively in ideas and symbols, and much of the effort of writing something down is expended on the task of transferring ideas from the chaotic realm of the mind to the orderly world of word and phrase. Nobody, least of all the writer, is able to identify the source of these ideas. They seem to emerge from a bottomless pit of the self where emotion and intellect converge to give expression to a voice within. We can probably assume that most successful creative writers have learned to tap into these two opposing facets of the cognitive self—emotion and intellect—and coax from them the coherent voice that gives birth to the writing self. Writing that lacks emotion is often sterile, barren. Writing without intellect is trivial, maudlin. However, all writing has at least one feature in common: for writing to take place the author must find the tools necessary to translate ideas into written symbols, which then exist—whether in clay, in stone, on paper, or in cyberspace—in some medium where others can potentially find, read, and draw meaning from them.

We are, of course, no closer to solving the mystery of where the writer's ideas come from. And though this is a fascinating question in itself, if I were to address it in the thorough manner it deserves, I would have no room left in which to address other questions. And so my primary concern in this chapter will remain the translation process, the sequence of steps the writer follows in order to move ideas from one medium (the mind) to another (the page, the computer screen).

All of the writing technologies we have looked at represent attempts to facilitate this process. They were devised to make it easier for writing and communication to take place. Some are simple refinements (the move from sheets to rolls of papyrus) while others represent technological breakthroughs that have had a profound impact on how people think and behave (the invention of moveable type). Today, a great deal of discussion is being devoted to the ramifications of electronic text on our writing habits and capabilities. I have already touched upon a number of these in the context of practical applications and everyday usages. However, in the following pages I wish to shift the discussion to a more philosophical plane.

What Writing Means

Humans are the only creatures on earth to have developed writing systems. If we were to look at history pragmatically, we could claim that writing as a technology emerged out of a perceived need, that is, to convey vital information in ways that simple orality did not allow. Every day of our lives we put writing to use in purely functional ways that make it possible for others to comprehend things that we already know. However, many hundreds of years ago the transcendent flexibility of language as a tool for conveying more than simple information was either discovered or recognized. In any event, someone, or perhaps many individuals over many years, came to understand that language could be used as a mode of personal expression, as a means of reaching inward rather than outward. Whether the need to express oneself found its realization in language, or whether language actually gave rise to that need, is hard to say now after the passage of centuries. All we can state for sure is that even after this discovery—even after people started writing their songs and poems—writing retained all its utilitarian functions. But, just as paint is used both as a chemical shield to protect wood and other surfaces from wind, rain, and sun, and also more extravagantly as a window on the soul, writing gained an aesthetic dimension that made it of value to an entirely different set of practitioners.

Once we have written something down, it can remain there for others to see as a lasting record of our thoughts. But what also remains there for others to see is the person, the self, the interior being, responsible for those words. Writing is a projection of the self, and creative writing is a projection of the private inner self. The words we use, every bit as much as the poems we write or the stories we tell, help to define who we are. This is because writing is about choice as much as it is about anything else. The creative writer lives in the same world from which we all derive our experience. And the writer is subjected to the same barrage of sensations—verbal, aural, visual—that all of us face each day. However, through a process of selective paring down and imaginative transmutation, the writer is able to use these sensations as raw material for art. This is a highly subjective process. No two people will choose exactly the same words to describe a similar event or to evoke the same emotional response. The choice is an expression of the individual. And in this sense we can see that the words we use—as soon as we make the decision to write them down—reveal who we are because they are a reflection of a personally exclusive point of reference from which we alone view the world.

> Writing in any form serves as both an extension and a reflection of the writer's mind. And each particular technology of writing...is a different form of projection, suggesting a somewhat different relationship between the written word and the mind. (Bolter 207)

I would take Bolter's argument one step further and suggest that writing technologies behave as metaphors for the mind. Just as we store words in our memory, we store them on paper or on computer disk. The process of recall is much the same in each case. We sift through our mind for a piece of stray text, a word, or a phrase, or we scrutinize indexes or we leaf through papers, or we scroll through a document on a computer screen. Each of these storage mediums varies in its capacity and reliability. And I would suggest that the medium of least reliability and narrowest storage capacity is the mind. This explains in part why other storage mediums were developed in the first place.

Like other means of artistic or personal expression, writing marks the convergence of the spiritual and the corporeal. It is an attempt to render articulate that which is fundamentally unintelligible and unknowable. Our desire to translate experience into literature springs from a profound urge to get to the bottom of ourselves and the role we are meant to play on this earth. The imagination helps us along the way, yet this too is something we can never hope to fully comprehend. The only elements we see are those which drift to the surface and find their expression in language; the murkier depths remain hidden from view, though they are hinted at in what we write. This is why so many works of the imagination—not only verbal ones—are startling and disorienting, even to the individual responsible for their coming into existence. The imagination does not operate in a logical or even rational manner; its movements cannot be charted. It will shift abruptly, making unexpected connections and sometimes even formulating innovative or revolutionary ideas. Drawing that which is alien and unforseen to the surface of consciousness is an essential function of the creative process.

The Role of the Author

Computer-based writing technologies offer us as writers new ways in which to relate to our texts. The progression from idea to written word on the computer is a fluid process, one free of the physical limitations imposed by pen, paper, and ink, as well as the terrifying blank page. Creative writers expend a good portion of their energies on revision, and on the computer this can be carried out automatically, instinctively, without the distraction and confusion of a great number of editorial symbols marring the printed page. Revision becomes not so much drudgery as a process of refinement as we sharpen our prose, or amend our poems, moving blocks of text from place to place, erasing entire lines with a single key stroke, inserting words with fluid ease.

> Writing is usually done sitting down and has nothing to do with heavy lifting; it is not considered a physical burden. Yet a certain amount of drudgery has always attached to the task of putting words on paper, and some writers have even attributed great importance to the physically resistant materials as they affect their writing consciousness. Word processing promises the removal of drudgery, and drudgery is usually associated with menial tasks connected with physical procedures. Word processing appears as a

liberating force, allowing unprecedented speed and convenience for the writer, precisely in that word processing is the computerization of the physical procedure. (Heim 192)

We have at our disposal an unaccustomed immediacy, a handy new conduit through which to channel our ideas directly from the chaos of the mind at work to the polished order of the printed page. "Speed and convenience" is a modern advertising refrain cited again and again as reason enough for using digitized contraptions such as video-cassette recorders, microwave ovens, and automatic bank tellers. The perpetual rush of modern urban life demands machines like these, with their nearly invisible interface, simply to keep us from falling too far behind. The machine sells itself and becomes immensely popular because with minimal training anyone can use it to perform a specific task and perform it competently. Many tasks, and not just writing, are completed faster and with less appreciable effort within the mechanized environment. Granted, as writers we are still occupied with the chore of filling the empty writing space with words, but on the computer this task does not require the writer to make physical contact with the writing space and to manually place the words there, one by one. A keyboard is not a pen; a keystroke is not comparable to act of using a hand-held writing implement to form a letter on a flat surface. It requires less effort because the keystroke for each symbol is exactly the same, regardless of the individual complexity of the symbol. Placing the word in the electronic writing space is a much more automatic gesture than writing it by hand. It requires less physical coordination and none of the conscious effort needed to construct each letter according to society's standards of legibility.

The same could be said of the act of writing using a typewriter as well. It is a mechanized process and, once again, the actual writing is accomplished with keystrokes instead of the hand. The keystrokes place uniform symbols on a page that, once the task is completed, can appear as clean and polished as a finished work. However, a typewritten page is much different from a page of electronically keyed text. Though each in its own way is simply a physical object, the typewritten page exists only on the corporeal plane of flesh and blood and ink and paper. The symbols are locked into place, having been positioned on the page by a small hammer meeting the writing surface through a ribbon of some ink-drenched medium. In order to change any of the symbols on that page, the intervention of a further physical medium, such as corrector tape or liquid paper, is necessary. If enough changes are needed, the page will have to be retyped, doubling the effort required to produce that single page of text.

By contrast, the electronic page of text retains much of the malleability of the idea as initially formulated in the author's mind. Each keystroke sets into motion an electronic impulse that evokes a combination of binary digits. These are translated on the computer screen as the symbols we read as text. However, this text remains fluid, in the sense that we can alter its appearance—make emendations, additions, deletions—without having to handle paper or pen or any other physically tangible object other than the keys on the keyboard. There is no physical permanence to electronic text, and the author is acutely aware of this, consciously or not, throughout the process of composition, not least because a power failure can mean permanent loss of data. Writers working in the electronic writing space are making changes to their text constantly. The process of revision takes place concurrently with that of composition. Words on the screen are not the same as words on the page. They represent a potential rather than a culmination. As long as it has not been locked into place on the printed page, text can be edited, ideas can be reformulated, meaning can be refined.

Because of these two features of computerized composition—easy passage from the mind to the screen and the fluid nature of digital text—the finished product of our efforts in the electronic workspace is no longer the sacred object it once was, as in the days when it was produced laboriously by hand or on the typewriter. With text produced on the computer, any interim draft will look very much like the finished text, and so the finished text is also potentially a working draft. Changes can easily be made and a new copy printed in a matter of minutes. As a result, it is entirely possible that we will view our texts more critically and accept radical emendations and suggestions for refinement more willingly than before.

This also means that in the electronic workspace the bond between writer and text is somewhat relaxed, allowing for the intervention of diverse critical voices as the text evolves. Electronic writing is therefore a more collaborative, more interactive, process than writing was in the days of pen and ink. The Romantic notion of the author as solitary tortured genius is being gradually eroded as computer technologies make it possible to create printed text easily, to store and circulate text in digital form on portable diskettes, and to transmit text over the networks. One is reminded of Scott Olsen's "mythic community."

> When written words are stored as electronic bits in memory, they are not objects to be owned. When authors are incarnated as electronic texts that can be erased, annotated, downloaded, linked, and redistributed, they are "textualized"; at that point their identities merge into a communal hypertext or discussion thread. (Sewell)

Writing in the electronic workspace appears then to define a revised role for the author with regard to the text, a role that is less one of authority or ownership, than it is one of custodianship.

> As long as the printed book remains the primary medium of literature, traditional views of the author as authority and of literature as monument will remain convincing for most readers. The electronic medium, however, threatens to bring down the whole edifice at once. It complicated our understanding of literature as either mimesis or expression, it denies the fixity of the text, and it questions the authority of the author. (Bolter 153)

If we take this argument a step further, we can see that electronic writing represents the ultimate liberation of the text from the author's influence. The writings of the French postmodernists, notably Roland Barthes and Michel Foucault, are often invoked when this aspect of electronic text is discussed. As a method of elucidating the text, the postmodernists pronounced the author to be dead, stating with emphatic certainty that the meaning of any text resides entirely within itself and that it is up to the reader to decide what meanings are relevant. The role of the author is reduced to a mere hack, someone who splatters words about on the page, infusing no more of his or her own soul into the work than would a mason building a brick wall or a child dabbling with a paint-by-numbers picture. The author is a compiler of influences and ideas from other places, times, and cultures who happens to mark the confluence of these ideas by placing them together on the page. That, however, is the full extent of the author's participation. From that point on it is the reader who must take control.

> Here we discern the total being of writing: a text consists of multiple writings, proceeding from several cultures and entering into dialogue, into parody, into contestation; but there is a site where this multiplicity is collected, and this site is not the author, as has hitherto been claimed, but the reader: the reader is the very space in which are inscribed, without any of them being lost, all the citations out of which writing is made; the unity of a text is not in the origin but in its destination, but this destination can no longer be personal: the reader is a man without history, without biography, without psychology; he is only that someone who holds collected into one and the same field all of the traces from which writing is constituted. (Barthes 54)

The text in its electronic form is the embodiment of this postmodernist concept because in an apparently real way it defies all efforts of the author to retain control over its destiny. It is elusive and transitory because it exists only as electrical impulses, which are not ours, or indeed anyone's, to have and to hold.

> Writing is now linked to sacrifice and to the sacrifice of life itself; it is a voluntary obliteration of the self that does not require representation in books because it takes place in the everyday existence of the writer. Where a work had the duty of creating immortality, it now attains the right to kill, to become the murderer of its author....In addition, we find the link between writing and death manifested in the total effacement of the individual characteristics of the writer; the quibbling and confrontations that a writer generates between himself and his text cancel out the signs of his particular individuality. (Foucault 117)

The view here would seem to be that by adopting an assumed voice and writing from the point of view of someone who is merely an invention—a fictional construct—writers deny their own existence and become, in fact, a party to their own annihilation. Expunged from the text, the writer is merely a scribe, recording the transactions of fictional characters or charting the flow of poetic ideas, but never actually placing him- or herself within the metaphorical field of vision between the reader and the text.

I have quoted enough sources to illustrate the prevalence of this view. However, I wish to draw a distinction.

The text itself, whether electronic or otherwise, is a physical object that, once written and distributed, is very much beyond the author's control. As we have seen, when it is liberated from the author's mind and placed into the hands of readers, the text assumes a life of its own. An electronic text is neither a solid nor a stable object. It can be altered in any number of ways by any number of readers. However, none of this changes the fact that the text is an intentional creation of the author. We can look at it, examine it, and think about it from different perspectives, but none of these will change the fundamental truth that the text exists only because the author intends it to exist. Even if the author removes him- or herself in body and spirit from the text and maintains a scrupulous objectivity with regard to the subject, the intention still remains. Even if the author removes his or her name from the written text, or repudiates it, or endeavours to destroy all copies, the intention still remains. As a corollary, we can therefore infer that in order to create a text, an author *must* have intention; without purpose there is no text, or, at any rate, none worth reading. Authorial intention animates the text, grants it a status on the continuum of written language higher than computer generated gibberish. The text becomes more than just words on a page or on a screen. And it doesn't matter if the author's intentions are ambiguous, or if the author formulates them as the writing progresses. Intention constitutes the moral and aesthetic perspective from which the story is told or the poem is written. It is embedded within the text. It is a direct message from author to reader, conveyed by means of story and character, image and word cluster. If it is present, the text lives, possibly much longer than the author; if it is not, the reader senses this and stops reading. Text without intention is an empty vessel that cannot hope to sustain the intelligent reader's interest; the text which lacks authorial intention withers and dies like a plant that has been sheared off at the roots.

It is pointless to deny the existence of the author in the text. The text will always be viewed in light of the author's necessary contribution. In the electronic writing space the reader may very well govern the text as physical object, but the author's intention remains paramount, because that is precisely what the reader is seeking. Over many years, the interpretation of any text may follow various and even divergent evolutionary paths, but intention remains the nexus in which the essential meaning resides.

We are persuaded by the language we speak to think of authors as authorities. But we also think that they are like other people, that they are humanly and historically representative. We think that they should be invisible, and that they are instrumental, that their opinions and personal lives should not get into the books they write, and that, when they do get into them, they undergo, together with their intentions, a process of translation or subversion. We think that a book is written by the language it shares with other books, and by the books which have preceded it. Nevertheless, the individual author continues to matter, in ways which suggest that we are also able to think of authors as inherently autobiographical, and, at the same time, as separate from the society which they represent and which wishes to honour them. (Miller 163)

The Role of the Reader

Without readers, a text is not called forth from the page and summoned into existence as a living thing; it is instead very much like the proverbial tree falling in the forest that makes no sound if nobody is present to hear it. Without a reader, the labour of the author comes to nothing. What has been created—whether a series of semantically linked symbols on paper or a text file residing as binary code on computer disk— remains where the author has placed it if no one bothers to initiate an act of reading and lift the symbols from the page—or goes to the trouble to call the file up from the disk to the screen—in order to actively engage the ideas residing therein. Because writing is inherently an act of communication, the reader is necessary in order for the act of writing to secure validity. Communication takes place the moment the reader begins searching for meaning within the text. And at that moment also the author's words cease to be his or her own. They undergo a singular transformation within a particular subjective consciousness over which the author has no control.

As an act of creation, reading is every bit as momentous and effective as writing. By looking into the author's text, the reader creates a text of his or her own. This process is otherwise known as interpretation. The reader encounters the text in much the same way that the musician encounters the score, fashioning a personal version based on signals, clues, and instructions provided by the author. Multiple readers create a multiplicity of texts, all of which vary in different ways from the author's original text. The author's intention, however, remains unchanged within the text—it is neither altered nor destroyed by the act of reading—to be discovered by some archetypical reader who may or may not even exist.

Writing is a solitary task, the author toiling alone, fashioning text out of ideas and symbols; but reading is a collaborative effort, one that links readers together with the author through the instrument of the text. Far from being the passive recipient of the author's words, the reader is in a continuous state of activity, questioning, considering, and ultimately deciding upon the exact nature of the relationship between author and reader. This is where the author forfeits control. Whatever intentions lie behind the creation of a particular text, the author cannot control the manner in which any individual reader receives and processes the text. In extreme cases

> the reader may well become the author's adversary, seeking to make the text over in a direction that the author did not anticipate. Adversarial reading is not new. One of the great advantages of writing in any medium is that readers can stop, reflect on a passage, and disagree. They can deliberately misread the text in the sense of imposing their own constructions that forcefully contradict the text. (Bolter 154)

Misreading has been going on for centuries, occurring most often in the past within a religious context. It has also had a profound impact on 20th-century morals, notably with regard to obscenity issues such as those which at one time surrounded works like

Ulysses and *Lady Chatterly's Lover*. However, more recently, misreading has continued to play a role in our lives, most memorably in the case of Rushdie's *The Satanic Verses*.

Electronic writing offers the reader the opportunity to exert even greater control over the text, and I am referring here to interpretive rather than physical control. The book has always been a "readerly," as opposed to a "writerly," object. Since a time shortly after the invention of movable type, authors, editors, and printers have been in the habit of providing markers and points of reference, such as page numbers, chapter headings, and indexes, as aids to guide the reader through the text. And readers have always been free to follow or ignore these markers as they choose. However, the presentation of text in its electronic form provides the reader with a more intimate type of access. The reader can enter the text, literally instead of figuratively. The reader can clip passages and move them elsewhere, or in other ways manipulate or alter the text. The reader is even able to mimic the function of the publisher and assume the task of distributing the text. The reader is also free to reformat the text in ways that are personally convenient or pleasing. Hypertext offers a literal demonstration of the control of the reader, because in hypertext,

> as in all electronic writing, the control of the presentation of text becomes part of the text itself, because the text consists not only of the words the author has written but also of the structure of decisions that the author creates and the reader explores. (Bolter 154)

However, it is not only within the framework of hypertext that the reader makes choices. All readers make choices every time they choose to read one text instead of another. The act of reading is itself a series of choices, whether to seek elucidation of the first text by consulting a second, whether to continue reading sequentially or to skip ahead, or to go back and re-read. Each choice that diverts the reader away from the author's design—each decision that causes the reader to stray from the path mapped out by the author—refashions the text in ways the author could not have anticipated. In hypertext the links and trajectories are embedded within the textual apparatus by the author; in traditional text the reader forges these on his or her own. But in both cases the result is a reading experience that is unlikely to be exactly duplicated by any other reader.

It is this interplay between reader and author that creates a literature. We read, we agree or disagree, and we are stimulated to compose a response (either in emulation or in opposition), and in effect reverse roles with the author. No written work ever emerges from a vacuum, without reference to another. Each text that is created represents an attempt to refine or refute or answer or in some way imitate or improve upon an earlier one. When viewed in this manner, all of our written literature—that which has come down to us from the past and that which is being created today—begins to look like an immense hypertextual structure feeding and building upon itself.

The Evolving Electronic Text

My understanding of an "evolving text" is of a written work as it is being formulated in the author's mind and finding its way to the page or the computer screen. Most writers are willing to discuss their methods of composition and talk openly about how an idea grew and expanded and eventually became the finished product that the reader finds inscribed on the pages of a book. They will speak of a period of gestation and perhaps remark upon how little the book or story or poem resembles the idea as originally conceived. They will also sometimes describe their writing habits, how long they work at a stretch, whether the morning, afternoon or middle of the night is the time most conducive to the flow of words and ideas. Eventually, the talk may come around to the physical practice of writing, the implements used to get the words down. This was rarely an issue in the past, when the matter may have centred upon the preferred type of pen. But with technology comes choice, and writers of the 19th and 20th centuries have been presented with an enormous array of equipment options.

This discussion brings several questions to mind. First, does how we write affect what we write? And second, if it does, is there any way to determine what those effects might be? Because all writers work differently, I cannot hope, within the scope of this volume, to arrive at definitive answers to either of these questions. What may be true of one writer will almost certainly have no bearing upon the habits of another. But I want to explore these questions nonetheless, if only to articulate the issues and to see if any generalizations do exist.

Jay Bolter tells us that

> Writing is the creative play of signs, and the computer offers us a new field for that play.
> It offers a new surface for recording and presenting text together with new techniques
> for organizing our writing. In other words, it offers us a new writing space. (10)

The emphasis here is placed most definitely on the word "new," in the sense that we began with of innovative and perhaps even revolutionary. As I stated above, the screen is quite different from the blank sheet, the pen different from the keyboard. However, "different" is about as far as this distinction can be taken. Qualitative assertions do not apply. It makes no sense to state generally and with absolute certainty that one writing tool is "better" than another. My earlier assertion that the degree of conscious effort required for composing on the computer is less than that required for composing by hand, though certainly true in general, does by no means lead inevitably to the declaration that writers who adapt themselves to the electronic writing space will produce better work. Such an estimate is purely subjective.

The mechanical gestures that comprise the act of writing come to us naturally, almost instinctively. At an early age we begin out of curiosity to reach and grasp, to take objects up in the hand and apply them to surfaces. Later on, the pen is taken up and gripped between the fingers and the thumb, and the words flow on to the page, the result of controlled protracted friction with a purpose. The writer bears witness to the page being filled with words, to inward thoughts being granted articulate voice. A special intimacy develops between the writer and the words on the page. The writer can touch the surface of them, feel the indentations that the pen has made as it rolled over the paper. A tangible sensation of accomplishment accompanies writing in long hand; a sense that something has been done that cannot easily be undone; a sense that something has been wrought, made, created, that did not exist before. There is physical effort involved also, the stress of flesh and bone bearing downward, of work being done. The process of revision raises different points. Deficient verses or passages of prose cannot simply be expunged. They must be crossed or scratched out, or actually torn away or excised with scissors. A word here and there can be stricken and another inserted above. But too many such casual emendations of this nature can render the manuscript illegible. And so the work must begin anew; the page must be rewritten, and in the process more changes will be made, passages will be omitted, others will be added or expanded, until the page is completed a second time. And then there it sits, the page full of words, something that can only be dealt with on a material level, an object that can be discarded or preserved but either way occupies physical space.

The permanent tangibility of the written word is not therefore under dispute. Once a word has been written it cannot be unwritten, it can only be crossed out or erased, or, for that matter, burned. However, it is conceivable that someone—perhaps a researcher or scholar—will find a way to decipher even a word that has been blotted out and thereby uncover the vestiges of an author's original design that did not survive intact in the completed work.

The written word also provides evidence of a different kind. In much the same way that a visual artist inscribes markings on paper or leaves painted depictions on canvas—what amounts to a personal imprint—the writer leaves written words on the page. The autograph is evidence of the author's own physical tangibility, evidence that the author is or was a human being much like ourselves. The personal signature is the stamp of authenticity, proof that this person exists, or once existed and actually held these papers or this book in hand, and is more than just a name on a title page or a face in a flyleaf photograph. For collectors of literary artifacts the autograph is valued above all else. Books bearing the author's signature sell on rare book markets at elevated prices and are commonly stored in darkened, secured, climate-controlled, inner sanctums within libraries. To understand the matchless worth of the autograph we need only call to mind the fact that just six examples of Shakespeare's handwriting are known to exist. The intrinsic value of these pen markings is quite literally beyond our comprehension.

Electronic writing goes a long way toward eliminating the physical drudgery associated with getting words down on paper. It is much less strenuous to tap away at a keyboard than it is to apply continuous pressure to a sheet of paper through fingers gripping a pen. For writers who may suffer from a debilitating condition or physical infirmity, the computer keyboard is a liberating implement because it frees them from the constraints and limitations imposed by the physical body. And actually, this is true for all writers. The computer removes the physical aspect of writing, makes it seem effortless. It also removes the immediately tangible result of writing, the page filled with words. As well, the computer eliminates that aspect of personal intimacy with the words being written, and in a way becomes the mediator between the author and the evolving text. By choosing to work in the electronic medium, the writer in effect takes a step back from the text and is placed in the position of spectator, watching the text fill space on the screen. A further mediator between author and text is the word processing software that governs format and display of the text. The instinctive interplay between writer, pen, and paper is now replaced by a highly conceptualized, programmed, learned task that makes numerous sensory demands on the writer every moment. A wrong keystroke can have disastrous results. Editing is no longer a simple matter of crossing out of words or phrases. The editing commands of any word processing package are very likely to be complex and obscure combinations of keystrokes, actions that may well be memorized with repetition, but which are neither natural nor necessarily logical.

On the computer, text is saved in files as electronically charged bits of binary data—codes, if you will—that make no sense to us without the machine to convert them back into legible script. The file as stored on the hard drive or floppy disk bears no markings of our own hand or, indeed, of any hand. Once rendered into machine-readable form it is no longer directly accessible. It is inscrutable, hidden from our eyes and mysterious to our senses. We are quite helpless to do anything with our text files on our own and depend upon the technology of the computer to seek them out and present them to us. And we trust in the machine to deliver up our text in exactly the same condition in which we entered it.

Thus the computer introduces a complex, multi-layered interface structure between the writer and the text: the storage medium, the machine itself with its arcane rituals and obscure mechanisms, and the operating system, so far removed from pen and paper. But many writers—and indeed, it seems the majority of writers, myself included—willingly accept this structure as a condition being able to exploit the conveniences of the new medium. In fact, so ingeniously is this structure designed that we hardly perceive it at all, even though it holds our own work at a distance from us, completely inaccessible were it not for the equipment and the electricity needed to run it.

As I noted earlier, the engineers responsible for the computer's internal architecture and the many refinements in computer technology of the last decade or so have pursued a goal of concealing from us the intricate complexity of these machines that most of us now use every day of our lives. Without the need to learn how the equipment processes our commands—just flick a switch, press a button—what we are left with is, very simply, a stimulating visual environment coupled with speed of operation and efficient use of workspace. The blinking cursor is an invitation to enter text, it draws us in and acts as a prompting device. It takes on a role as the tip of an electronic pen, but it glides across the screen seemingly on its own, without anyone pushing it, moving with a precise, effortless flow, leaving words in its wake. The immediacy of this process is evident to anyone who has written using a computer. If we wish to revise, we may do so directly on the screen, without taking the disruptive interim step of producing a printout and editing by pen. It is possible to produce a finished document without once resorting to paper or "hard" copy. It is sometimes a contest for our thoughts to keep up with our words, and in fact the entire experience of word processing can assume the feel of a sport, in which the screen becomes the field of play.

> The accelerated automation of word processing makes possible a new immediacy in the creation of public, typified text. Immediacy is the sense of there being...no instrumental impediment to thinking in external symbols, only a...pure transparent element. As I write, I can put things directly in writing. My stream of consciousness can be paralleled by the running flow of the electric element. Words dance on the screen. Sentences slide smoothly into place, make way for one another, while paragraphs ripple down the screen. Words become high-lighted, vanish at the push of a button, then reappear instantly at will. Verbal life is fast-paced, easier, with something of the exhilaration of video games. (Heim 152)

Some of what Heim says can, of course, be applied to handwriting. However, even very rapid and tidy handwriting cannot begin to approximate the speed and accuracy of word processing, the clean legibility of an instantaneous product, the simple ease of electronic editing, the apparent miracle of devices such as "spell-check." Again, convenience and ease of use are reason enough to take advantage of the new technology. In a hectic world where time is quite literally a precious commodity, the desire for convenience and simplicity exerts a strong influence—stronger, perhaps, than we might think—over the choices we make.

But does the medium of production affect the product itself? Are writers who work in the electronic environment producing something different than they would have had they remained in the realm of pen and ink? There can be little doubt that computerized applications affect the process of writing. But how can we ever determine if the manner in which the words find their way onto the page actually has a tangible impact on the words themselves? According to Marshall McLuhan the medium is the message, or, less aphoristically, the mode of discourse governs the substance of that discourse. But little is certain in the misty realm of artistic creation. A more appropriate reply to these questions may be that all writers respond to the electronic environment in a manner that is highly individual, incorporating any benefits that may derive from the new electronic tools into their ingrained habits and creative rituals. Interesting and profitable studies might someday be conducted on authors who began working with electronic text well into their writing careers, comparing the work produced before to the work produced after the acquisition of computerized writing equipment.

As part of an effort to allow practising writers to speak for themselves, I have elicited some comments on this topic from some of the writers who subscribe to CREWRT-L.

Teresa L. Howard remarks,

> From the time I can remember, I've always loved long-hand, and painstakingly would write and rewrite poetry, short stories just to see the graceful strokes of black and white. I still compose most poetry in long-hand before taking it to the computer; however, when it comes to getting thoughts down on paper, the computer has greatly changed how I compose and edit material. I always hated typewriters, but I love the swiftness of the computer/wordprocessing, and rewriting is no longer a "groaner."

In a similar vein, Karen Ballentine states,

> When I write poetry, I still write with good old pen...and ink, but I revise my poems on the computer because once I have the meat of the poem down it helps my creativity to...be able to play with line breaks and such and see almost immediately if the revisions work.

Speaking in defence of traditional methods, Paul Cassidy maintains, "I still like to write by hand. The flow from brain to hand to paper is cleaner, more true, and uninterrupted. To me, a computer breaks the flow." And Cher A. Holt-Fortin avers, "I still write longhand and then put it on the computer and then revise on hardcopy. Something about the kinesthetics of pen and paper and ink. Can't just create on the tube."

To others, the computer furnishes significant benefits. Eric Crump admits, "I feel in love with word processing because it afford[s] grace and flexibility and speed and let[s] me spew forth words with ease" ("Writing on..."). Karen Alkalay-Gut appreciates that "The possibility of 'seeing things clearly'—of being able to revise provisionally and test out these revisions against each other—has allowed me not only to open up my writing, but my thinking as well." Jennifer Sader, however, sounds a note of caution when she says,

> I've noticed that writing on a computer makes it more difficult to find a "finish line," to know when a poem is done. That's one of the things that has helped me improve, however, because it's much easier to revise. Sometimes, it's hard to leave a poem alone, though, because it's so easy to switch around a line, redo the ending, etc.

And Brian McKinney echoes this concern:

I have a minor problem with computer writing in that it is sometimes too easy to shovel words onto the screen. I keep thinking about Samuel Beckett, who wrote in French to force himself to make conscious choices of every word he used.

Obviously, there is no consensus on this point, nor is it reasonable to expect one. Writers, like people engaged in other trades, will search for the most efficient way to get the job done and will naturally seize upon the technology that offers the least resistance to their efforts. This is only practical. And if the quality of the writing is high—and the writer is satisfied with it—then it is possible that the means by which the words found their way on to the page is irrelevant.

Nevertheless, as we have seen, computer technologies *have* had a profound impact on our work habits and, by shifting attention away from the product to the process, have made us much more conscious of what we are doing when we write. The word on the screen is not the same tangible, stubbornly unyielding object as the word on the page, and we neither regard nor treat it as such. On the computer, we are less attached to the word as a fixed, immutable object; we alter our words and let them go with fewer sighs of regret. And this is because the act of putting them there is not as strenuous. Our sweat is not as apparent. The machine comes close to creating the illusion that words flow unimpeded from the brain to the screen. It invites us to interact with our evolving text on a dynamic, intimate, immediate level. The machine *responds* to our commands—it *does* what we tell it to do—something the blank piece of paper will never learn. As we work and grow familiar with it, the keyboard, like the pen, becomes an extension of our will. The word processing command language becomes internalized; we forget to even think about it. Because they are available to us almost instantly, the reality of our words being stored in the belly of the computer as incomprehensible bits of data seems beside the point. Oblivious to the technical intricacies and thankful that we have no need to worry about them, we continue to write, creating our fictional worlds and constructing our poems from material furnished by the world around us. Language is our real tool. The computer merely makes it easier for us to manipulate it. And as we do so the human-computer interface gradually melts away, and we become one with the machine.

Where Do We Go From Here?

Many of us can still remember learning penmanship in grade school; the hours spent tracing letters with a pencil in imitation of a faultlessly inscribed example held out to us to emulate. The effort expended on such exercises was not wasted because we wrote everything in longhand as we grew up. We passed in our finished assignments on sheets of lined looseleaf bearing written symbols laboriously inscribed in our own hand. As we entered university, perhaps in the late 1960s or early 1970s, chances are we acquired a typewriter, to ease the physical travail of scholarly endeavour, to speed our writing, and also to satisfy the higher standards of teachers who demanded typewritten work. The people of my generation did not become closely acquainted with computers until the late 1970s or early 1980s, and at that time their use was restricted mainly to the sciences. Humanities scholars began to see computers infiltrate their workspace in the mid-1980s. And now, as we pass the midpoint of the last decade of the century, computers are everywhere. They have taken up permanent residence beside us in our homes, they have moved into our offices and our schools. They regulate a great many of our activities, and—quietly and screened from view—have made themselves indispensable.

> How many of us will still be writing with a pen in the next century? In the 22nd century, how many people will actually know what a pen is for? These questions may seem facetious, but we need only think back to our parents, who had inkwells on their school desks, to realize that the answers are not obvious. Fifty years ago, writing could only be done in a special environment: the ballpoint pen was unknown, "fountain" pens could be unreliable, the only medium for "writing" was paper. With only a few exceptions, a "writer" produced "manuscripts," and typewriters were for two fingered newspaper reporters, and secretaries. (Coniam)

In the last thirty years the writer's desktop has been transformed from a technological backwater into a sophisticated office space replete with advanced communications, publishing, and writing devices and systems. The computer seems to fall naturally within the writer's domain because of its capacity to store, manipulate, and display large blocks of textual information. Indeed, the personal computer has very quickly become the "essential" tool of the writer's trade, largely superseding pen, ink, and the typewriter in little more than a decade. It would seem reasonable to venture that most people under a certain age—say, fifty—are familiar with some computer operations, and that the lower the age range the greater the degree of familiarity. However, what we are witnessing today, as David Coniam observes, is the complete usurpation of most of our working and learning spaces by computer technologies. In the classroom, children are being introduced to computers either at the same time they encounter conventional writing tools, or else instead of conventional writing tools. Coniam argues that children who acquire their writing skills on computers will benefit from a greater facility with language since they will bypass the labour-intensive step of learning how to form each letter by hand, a process that he sees as a barrier to language itself. Though it is unlikely that handwriting will ever disappear totally, it is possible that in very few years "penmanship" in the classroom environment will be reduced in significance to little more than a physical exercise intended to sharpen motor skills and stimulate hand-eye coordination. "Real" writing will take place at the keyboard, where children will be freed of the physical limitations imposed by their own bodies, limitations that may actually stand in the way of learning how to play with words and impede the process of internalization that is a vital part of mastering any language.

The keyboard is an obvious visual palette from which the child can see and choose the letters he wants to write with. And even though the QWERTY keyboard layout is not user-friendly...these factors have little impact on early child writing. The overriding factor for a child is not speed or efficiency, that is, but simply the labour required to produce the characters. The easier it is for the writer to make letters, the more letters will be made. (Coniam)

Is it possible that handwriting will go the way of Latin and Greek—forced from the centre to the periphery of knowledge by more urgent and fashionable subjects of study—and become a quaint or esoteric skill of some historical interest but of little or no practical importance to daily life? I bring this up because of my earlier discussion concerning the enduring fondness with which some writers still regard their own handwritten words. If we are indeed witnessing the demise of handwriting, then our generation may be one of the very last to consider pen and ink a viable option when undertaking a writing project. The generation of writers just now starting school will almost certainly grow up and attain maturity with a whole different set of assumptions regarding the written word, regarding language, and regarding the uses to which these may be put.

As Richard Lanham says, "The students we teach are going to do most of their writing and much of their reading on an electronic screen. They are going to live—they live now—in a world of electronic text" (121).

It has been said that we live in an "information age." That is, we live at a time when information as a commodity drives a good portion of the international economy and is something that is bought and sold and consumed, like wheat or automobiles. Information itself used to be text-based and used to be transferred physically from place to place, printed on pieces of paper. Yet today these notions seem like something not just from the recent past, but from the long past, like the horse and buggy. Computers offer a range of possibilities, two of which are the incorporation of many types of media into our documents and the ability to duplicate them endlessly and send them instantly around the globe. Hypermedia systems allow us to insert sounds and still or moving pictures within our works. Electronic tools have made the concept of the "document" much more complex than it used to be. Many students are no longer required to "pass in" their term "papers" and instead give their instructors electronic work on computer disk. This was novel a few years ago. But it is almost passé now as more and more students deliver their assignments as electronic mail. Computer technologies have constantly thwarted our attempts to define their capabilities and to anticipate where they will take us next. And without a direct link to the future, this is unlikely to change.

But I expect books will not disappear. They will endure in close proximity to the new technology. The same material will be available in a variety of formats, either locally or online. There will be more ways to access information and acquire knowledge.

There will be more ways to learn. "Ten years from now, teenagers are likely to enjoy a much richer panorama of options because the pursuit of intellectual achievement will not be tilted so much in favor of the bookworm, but instead cater to a wider range of cognitive styles, learning patterns, and expressive behaviors" (Negroponte 220).

4

Implications: Issues of Storage and Retrieval

An electronic book does not join itself to other books end to end, as printed books do when we set them on a shelf. Instead, the electronic book can merge into a longer textual structure at a thousand points of contact; it can dissolve into constituent elements that are constantly redefining their relationships to elements in other books. An electronic book is not as vigorous in asserting its identity over [or] against all others in the world's libraries. It invites exploration as part of a vast network of writings, pointing the reader both to itself and to other books. Electronic writing therefore breaks down the familiar distinctions between the book and such larger forms as the encyclopedia and the library.

Jay Bolter, *Writing Space* 87-88

The book—the commonly recognized incarnation of pages and covers that exists today—is, quite simply, a masterpiece of accumulated innovation and technical refinement. It is one of our society's most ingenious, not to mention popular, artifacts, cleverly combining craftsmanship, science, and art. Apart from its content, the "book" is an object, one you can hold in your hand and admire. Its appeal derives in part from its apparent simplicity, its balanced appearance. Opening a book is one of the easiest things in the world to do. You flip the cover back and the contents display themselves, page after page. There is no interface to learn, no command language to master. A book as an object has no secrets. Nothing is hidden from view. Each page can be accessed immediately, with almost no effort. Even when its covers are closed it retains this immediate accessibility because books are *about* access. They exist in their present form in order to make words, illustrations, diagrams, charts—anything that can be printed on paper—accessible.

Most often, a book is constructed in accordance with aesthetic principles; it can serve both practical and ornamental functions simultaneously. Many of its individual details—the binding, the paper, the illustrations, the cover, the typeface—result from decisions that have been arrived at with the ultimate goal in mind, one hopes, of making the finished product as appealing, as inviting, and as attractive as possible. In a competitive marketplace, few publishers will be willing to commit funds to the creation of an unsightly product. And authors want readers to be drawn to their books, not repelled by them. They want their readers to have as many reasons as possible for entering the worlds they have created. Presumably, in this regard, an aesthetically pleasing design would be an asset rather than a liability.

However, the book is more than just the sum of its tangible components. It does not exist simply to join paper, cardboard covers, and colour illustrations together into a happy union. The book as we know it today represents the most convenient medium yet devised for the storage of human knowledge. Virtually unchanged for hundreds of years, the book has never encountered a serious challenge for its position as the universal format of choice for the presentation of text. We can enter our libraries this very day and easily locate books that were produced as long ago as 500 years or more, manufactured in countries that have not existed for centuries. Except for the nature of the binding, and perhaps a few minor physical details, they present their text in exactly the same manner as the books we find displayed in the new-release section of our local bookstore. Any changes that have occurred are merely refinements.

Moreover, the physical design of books makes them easy to store and tempting to accumulate. Except in large numbers, they are not inconvenient to own. Most people are able to retain at home a collection of their favourite texts, and for other, perhaps rare or expensive items, there is always the library. For most of us the sum total of human knowledge is readily available. This would not be possible without the book in its present form.

Books also exist on a more elevated plane and occupy an exalted position in the annals of human history. And this is because, though a book may appear to some to be simply an object, what we really cherish about any single book has much more to do with the words printed on its pages than with its physical components. A book occupies something other than just physical space. It occupies a more abstract form of intellectual or philosophical space. We can speak of a book being about something; we can say a book has meaning, that it contains ideas. And ideas can be influential, or trivial, or even dangerous. Ideas can alter the course of history. For this reason a book does not reside in our world in quite the same way that other objects do. For example, its bulk has nothing to do with its significance; the elaborate decorative details of its cover design have no bearing on its ultimate value, which may not become apparent for centuries. Books can assume an emotionally or intellectually significant role in an individual's life. They can inflame people to excessive displays of emotion, to protest loudly and argue at length, to take the measure of their convictions and unite behind or against a cause. People have been jailed and condemned to death because of the books they have written. Books do more for us than just convey information or tell a good story. They take us out of ourselves and our immediate surroundings and allow us to comprehend people we could never possibly meet and cultures we will never experience. They symbolize knowledge, and something beyond knowledge. Wisdom, perhaps.

The book also represents a tangible connection to the past, to other times, other places, other people. It forges a direct link to a shared intellectual heritage and binds us all closer together in a community of understanding. However, the book is also a private place, a closed and finite space, self-contained and self-referential. A book may refer to or be "about" other books, but when it comes into our hands it proclaims its existence as an independent cognitive unit. This intellectual autonomy is perhaps the most endearing feature of the book, the one that enables us to regard the book as a world unto itself into which the reader can retreat. Its boundaries are clear and indisputable; its covers demarcate and distinguish its contents from those of all other books. There is nothing ambiguous about where one book ends and another begins, about which pages reside within what covers. The configuration of the book leaves nothing to chance.

This romantic and somewhat figurative conception of the book has traditionally had a practical utility as well. The physical unity of the book allows it to be described in an absolute fashion, allows its contents to be analyzed and classified. Accessibility of knowledge depends to a great extent upon indexing and codification systems. And the convenience for classification purposes of having knowledge available in discrete and digestible segments has greatly enhanced the modes of access that we have seen evolve. There is nothing random about the order in which books are placed on library shelves. A great deal of intellectual effort is expended to ensure that every book takes up residence in the one spot most appropriate to its subject matter. The primary concerns of those whose job it is to classify items according to subject are that the logic of the classification scheme be adhered to, and that the book be easily located on the shelf. Classification systems such as that devised many years ago for use at the Library of Congress generally place books on similar subjects close beside one another, although the business of classification is not usually this simple. The Library of Congress system, to remain with that example, is distinguished by its browsability. Though the intricacy and complexity of this classification scheme ensures that very little is left to chance, it does make browsing not just possible, but advisable. Anyone involved in advanced research will readily cite the blessings of serendipity. Often a "found" book will turn out to be the best book of all.

The electronic book, together with other forms of electronic text, do not fit so neatly into traditional categories. They are elusive for the simple reason that they are not manifest as physical objects that we can scrutinize and examine, and to which we can point with unerring confidence. As I stated earlier, electronic text is fluid and malleable; many copies can be generated and distributed at the touch of a key; and they can be altered in ways the author never imagined. Stored remotely, electronic text travels along wires, only emerging into view upon reaching the computer screen. In the absence of the technology needed to make it visible, electronic text remains hidden away and every bit as indecipherable and arcane as the lost language of a defunct society, as intangible as the future. We may wish to ask how we can entrust our great works of literature—those now in existence and those still to be written—to a medium that has every appearance of ephemerality, that so openly challenges our notions of permanence.

In the following sections I wish to explore some of the issues surrounding electronic text as a means of preserving our cultural heritage and to look at how libraries may best deal with the challenges it poses.

The Object Itself: Electronic Text as a "Thing"

We live in a tactile world, bound to it by sensory perception. What we see and hear and feel and taste and smell fills our lives and makes us complete. In the course of living from day to day we deal with objects that appeal to some or all of our senses. We are accustomed to being able to pick things up and examine them. A book, for example, will first impinge upon our senses visually. Then we lift it and feel its weight and the texture of its pages, hear the paper as it flips past our fingers. Many books emit a detectable odour; and, if one were so inclined to investigate closely, could be found to possess a distinctive flavour as well.

Concrete objects of this nature are relatively easy for us to control and manage. We can find a place for them and retrieve them whenever they are needed. We can name them and show them to others. And we can refer to them in the context of living our lives because the name provides a conceptual framework that acts as a stimulus to our senses even in the absence of the object itself. We would probably be surprised to learn how much of our conversation is devoted to the discussion of objects that are not present, and—equally—how profoundly we react to these names as we conjure in our minds the corresponding sensory image.

Electronic text does not easily lend itself to this mode of categorization, primarily because it is difficult for our brains to separate it from the medium in which it is stored. Despite the prevalence of computer technology in our lives—and the electronic digital impulses that are its lifeblood—we still have trouble conceiving of something that retreats completely from the sensual field of play as an "object." An electronic text file residing on computer disk takes up no space in our lives, even though the disk itself does. The file does not declare itself visually or in any other manner as something to be put away or valued or maintained. In its absence, it cannot be referred to verbally except in the abstract. It cannot even be displayed by the computer in its entirety; only a single screen at a time can be delivered before our eyes as evidence of its existence. And if we try to examine electronic text away from the computer that decodes it, we will find no trace whatever of its existence: a computer disk that contains text looks and feels to us the same as a computer disk that contains no text at all. We could say that an electronic book exists only when it is open. Close it, and your fingers will grasp air.

Much the same could, of course, be said of cassette tapes containing music and video tapes containing sounds and moving images, or the digital equivalents of sound and image stored, like text, on disk. Regarded simply as objects apart from the devices that read them, all tapes and disks look the same to us whether anything is stored on them or not. In their digital format, even music and images can be held at one site and accessed from another. They can be transferred and duplicated instantly. However, electronic text is in many ways unique. It can engage the reader at a level of interactivity unmatched by any other magnetically stored entertainment or communication. Unlike other computer files such as programs or sounds or images which must maintain a degree of integrity in order for the machine to properly read and decode them, electronic text files can be easily altered, changed beyond recognition, retrieved, edited, downloaded, searched, merged or linked with other e-texts. Many of us encounter electronic text on a daily basis, yet because it eludes the most immediate of our senses, it remains remote from our experience. We confront it at one remove, through the distorting prism of the machine.

It is perhaps this perception of shadowy insubstantiality that has so far prevented electronic text from achieving widespread acceptance and utility as a medium of publication. We associate publication with the "thing": the book, the journal. Publication implies permanence, which to most of us denotes words printed on a paper medium, words that will be around for years to come, that we can consult at our leisure, that we can touch and hold. There persists in the minds of many readers a sentimental concept of the "book" as something "warm and fuzzy," something that provides comfort, that we can take to bed and pass from one generation to the next. Somehow, electronic text does not inspire in the reader a comparable bond of intimacy. It fails to trigger the affectionate response that normally accompanies the concept of "book." And it lacks the cluster of metaphorical and emotional associations that over hundreds of years have accumulated around the book as a social construct. The book has penetrated so deeply into and become so firmly rooted in our collective consciousness that even the most progressive and open-minded of us resist thinking of it in any but its present form. It is a misguided and likely futile effort to appropriate the feel of the traditional book that has given rise to the misnomer "electronic book." For a digital text file is by no means the same as a book, though it has the potential to become a book. We approach it differently and put it to different uses. It is at once more and less than a book, depending on how you choose to look at it.

Clearly, we have to begin revising how we think about electronic text. By confining the discussion to the terminology of print culture we rob ourselves of the opportunity to grow and change with the new technology. Electronic text is not a fad that is going to fall into disuse tomorrow or next week when something better comes along. Present trends indicate that electronic text will continue every day to weave its way more intricately into the fabric of our lives. As computer literacy spreads so will electronic text. We must be prepared to deal with the challenge it presents.

An appropriate place to begin facing up to this challenge is the library. Librarians are in the main pro-active. They have traditionally been prepared to embrace change and to alter procedures and policies in order to accommodate new formats. However, electronic text poses a special and potentially difficult challenge, not least because of the equipment demands that accompany any attempt to either house or identify works in electronic form and which introduce budgetary as well as technical considerations. It is not enough to simply purchase and store electronic texts. They must be made accessible and available as well. A dilemma facing the library world at the present time revolves around the question of how far to pursue this notion of availability. Should electronic texts be treated the same as printed texts and be "shelved" for patrons to remove and take home and use as best as they are able? Or do the responsibilities of the library extend to providing exhaustive reference assistance to patrons wishing to consult these items? What is the justification for handling text in electronic form differently than text in print form? This issue has sparked a lively debate in the literature, a debate that is not likely to be quickly resolved when one considers that the leaps by which technology is advancing almost daily have cast a shadow of doubt over a fundamental concept with regard to library collections: ownership.

Libraries are now able to provide electronic access to materials not physically housed on site, electronic texts that cost nothing but which every day are escalating in value and significance for the researcher. Electronic journals, once on the margins of scholarship, have become mainstream, as demonstrated by the recent acquisition of *Postmodern Culture* by Oxford University Press. There are increasing pressures being brought to bear on library acquisition managers to add electronic materials to their collections and subscription lists. However, the need to somehow maintain inventories of electronic materials means that libraries are being called upon to perform functions normally associated with the campus computer facility, that librarians are finding they require the technical expertise necessary to deliver electronic journals on demand, to expeditiously navigate the Internet, the World Wide Web, and other networks, as well as to continue to support the many online and CD-ROM bibliographic and full text databases currently in use.

The provision of information is becoming an ever more complex activity, and we are seeing a shift in the role that libraries and librarians are being expected to play. Adeptness in computer applications is no longer an elective skill. Systems evolve and proliferate, each one different from and more sophisticated than the last. As demand for these services escalates, exploring electronic tools and resources has come to constitute a major portion of many librarian's duties.

And it is entirely reasonable that this should be the case. Libraries exist, in the words of Crawford and Gorman, "to give meaning to the continuing human attempt to transcend space and time in the advancement of knowledge and the preservation of culture" (3). When that attempt is made using an electronic rather than a print technology, this is no reason for libraries to stop supporting "the advancement of knowledge and the preservation of culture." However, there remains a need to coolly appraise what is being accomplished with any new technology, to assess its value and study its potential. It is foolish to commit scarce resources to expensive projects simply because they exploit technology that is new and trendy.

What are the advantages of electronic text? What are its weaknesses? And how should libraries approach it?

The electronic text as a "thing" remains, as we have seen, within the belly of the machine, aloof from the user, or reader. It occupies space only in the sense that, as a series of electrical impulses, it alters the molecular structure of the surface of a magnetic medium. In order for us to be able to interact with it on a meaningful level, the electrical impulses must be conveyed to some sort of display unit and translated into symbols we can understand. We take in text through our eyes, and it is here—where the technology touches us physically—that its vulnerability is exposed and its weaknesses revealed.

Reading is a fundamental human activity which benefits all individuals and all of society. More adamantly, "Sustained reading leading to the acquisition of knowledge *is* important and *is* good for the individual and for society" (Crawford and Gorman 14). And, as we all know, this activity has been universally stimulated by the manufacture of high-quality print products. Still, there have been many published prognostications which foresee the end of print as a viable technology and predict, with varying degrees of exactness and certainty, that in coming years people will be reading everything on a computer screen. Equally, there have been a great many articles devoted to the subject of the library's role in a future in which print technology has been largely superseded. Some see the library as an irrelevance, a holdover from a bygone era; others regard libraries as vital for the continuance of civilization. Regardless of what people think, however, and as long as library collections are dominated by print, the fate of libraries probably depends to a large degree upon people continuing to read print on paper. And this does not appear to be something that most of us will stop doing anytime soon, at least not willingly.

> Print is not dead. Print is not dying. Print is not even vaguely ill. Despite the best efforts of those who predict (and have predicted for many years) that print-on-paper is due to be replaced in the near future, there are no objective reasons to believe that this is so. (Crawford and Gorman 14)

Walt Crawford and Michael Gorman, in their book *Future Libraries: Dreams, Madness & Reality*, place strong emphasis on the point that the book as a technology was successful and has remained popular for hundreds of years for the very simple reason that it is masterful at doing what it was designed to do, that is, preserve printed words so that people can read them. "The facts are that books work and they work better than any alternative for *sustained reading*" (Crawford and Gorman 17-18). Even after years of improvements and refinements in the field of electronic text display, the book remains the appropriate technology for presenting large blocks of text in such a way that people can immerse themselves in words on the page for lengthy periods. And it is only through "sustained reading" that understanding occurs and knowledge is acquired.

Electronic text is not without its advantages and we have already touched upon one clear advantage that electronic text enjoys over its print predecessor. However, the primary feature of electronic text that makes it the preferred format in some cases is its fluid nature. Once converted into digital form, text can be transported across vast distances at the touch of a key, and it can be edited and adapted with astounding ease. It is excellent for conveying information in small bites that can be read and digested quickly. As an editorial tool it is unsurpassed. Most printed books are now produced from text that, at one point or another, was stored in digital form. And this is because the "evolving text" when it is available electronically is elastic and malleable, a feature that is of extraordinary benefit in the editorial process.

I have been emphasizing the role of electronic text as a stage in a process, a temporary medium that eventually gives way to the durable and unalterable format of print. And despite the fact that electronic journals continue to proliferate at an astounding rate, this is still by and large the case. For example, those of us receiving a great volume of email messages daily print out any we wish to preserve. I am working in an electronic environment at the moment, but when this volume attains its final form, it will see the light of day in print. I want my words to be as easy to read as possible, and for this reason I am not yet prepared to distribute them solely in digital form. Undertakings in electronic text conversion such as Project Gutenberg notwithstanding, the fact remains that not all computer monitors or display devices are easy to read and virtually none are easy to read for long stretches. Electronic text is certainly flexible, but because it depends so heavily upon a technology that is still evolving, print on paper reserves for itself the advantage of readability. The fact that electronic text is not as easy to read as printed text represents a severe obstacle to widespread acceptance that in all likelihood will not be overcome until well into the next century, if ever.

How does this affect the many forecasts that see the "virtual library" as imminent? In practical terms, I regard the concept of a library housing nothing but electronic documents to be one of pure conjecture, a product of the imaginative fancy of futurists. This is not to say that it will never happen, but at the moment even the instruction manuals for the machines we purchase in order to make use of electronic text are only available in printed form. And I would ask quite seriously too if the "virtual library" is something we should even be striving for. Just because something *can* be done does not necessarily mean it *should* be done or that we should petition for it to be done. Neither does it mean that we should dispense with previous methods for accomplishing the same tasks. Crawford and Gorman argue very strongly that technology should be used appropriately, to solve targeted problems or to make specific types of work simpler or easier, and not in a whimsical fashion that would see it applied wherever an application happens to be found.

Still, what we are leaving further and further behind is a time that most of us can still remember, if only vaguely: the days when print-based sources of information were the *only* sources of information. As more material is converted into machine-readable form—and, indeed, many essential items are being released *only* in machine-readable form—scholars and researchers find they are required to consult this type of material with greater frequency. Librarians are often expected to know about, and rapidly become conversant with, new textual and graphical formats before they are commonplace or even widely available. Far from rendering libraries and librarians obsolete, electronic text promises an array of new opportunities for librarians who are willing to confront the challenge of each new format as it arrives on their desks.

Storage and Archiving

For centuries, books and printed journals have been home to both major and minor literary figures, their pages filled with the efforts of the celebrated and the obscure. The literature of nations endures on such pages within bound volumes shelved in libraries around the world. Libraries everywhere maintain exact and detailed records of their holdings, as much to provide access as to keep accurate inventories so that needless duplication is avoided. Libraries are widely perceived as cultural repositories, home for an ever-expanding body of knowledge. We look at our own library and see the building—a space defined by walls and windows. We see the collection—a growing yet finite number of books and journals, video and audio tapes, CD-ROMs. Given the volume of material to be found in most research libraries, one would expect that any book or journal article or piece of information could be obtained locally. But this is not always the case, and scholars frequently discover that they must consider materials held in many libraries in order for their research to be comprehensive. To aid in the research process libraries formed a functional network many years ago, a network of interlibrary communication that allows each to tap the resources of all others. Library collections are defined by walls, but are not confined by walls. Libraries that participate in what has expanded into a global interlibrary loan system collectively form a library without limits whose patrons have access to a world of material, a currency of scholarly exchange, by which we normally mean books and journals. These materials are borrowed and loaned in accordance with regulations that may vary from place to place, but which tend to emphasize a single universal concept, one that has formed the basis of library collecting and lending policies for hundreds of years: ownership.

Books are curious objects because in one respect they can be owned, and yet in another they can never be owned. Ownership signifies control; if you own something, then presumably you control who uses it, when, and for how long. Libraries are complex institutions, operated by librarians and governed by rules designed to facilitate access and provide service to a wide range of user groups. They enforce control over the items in their collections using a variety of restrictions and regulations—loan periods, fines for overdues, security systems to discourage theft—and in this way endeavour to ensure that the information contained within their walls is available perpetually. However, the library controls only the physical unit, the book itself, often a single copy. The content ranges far and wide, liberated from its prison of pages by the act of reading. It can be reproduced—likely stripped to its essentials—during a simple conversation, or it can form the basis of a lecture and be imparted to many individuals in a single recitation. The book remains in the library, but the ideas expressed in its pages circulate uninhibited throughout the scholarly community, providing the focus for a discourse that will thrive for as long as those ideas are perceived as cogent and vital, or until they are superseded by new ideas.

Yet the traditional perception—that books are both owned and controlled—persists in the minds of many. The physical object is after all something that can be tagged and traced. However, the sort of control that libraries are mostly in the business of exerting over the materials in their collections is "bibliographic" control. Bibliographic control is most obviously manifest in the subject headings and call numbers assigned to individual items, labels that define those items uniquely within the collection and which make the identification and retrieval of those items a matter of uncomplicated ease. Patrons can quickly locate and determine the availability of any library item. This is because library materials have traditionally fallen into the category of tangible "things" that can be identified, touched and borrowed. Even a CD-ROM, though its function is to deliver text to a computer screen, is an item with both a location and usage restrictions.

Pure electronic text does not conform with tradition. As Mary Goodyear observes,

> Information used to be stored on printed pieces of paper. Pieces of paper can only be at one place at one time—essentially controlling access to that information. Physical access was required for intellectual access....Today, information stored in electronic form can be easily accessed from thousands of miles away. Exact copies can be made without the owner of the original losing his or her copy or even knowing it has been shared with another person. (25)

A unique and (for librarians) troubling feature of electronic text is that it refuses to honour library walls and security systems the way books do. Instead, it flows freely, in most cases unrestricted. Libraries do not have to retain copies on site in order to provide access. In fact, with more and more people tapping into remote sites and retrieving texts from home, some would argue that libraries are not needed at all.

> Electronic books mean that libraries need not keep large and expensive stores of bulky and decaying paper. Libraries can shrink from large warehouses to small rooms....Libraries will not need to buy multiple copies to allow for...book destruction. Nor will they need binderies to bind journals or magazines into volumes, or to rebuild old books. Nor will they need shelvers. (Rawlins)

Personally, given the great cultural and scholarly diversity of materials stored there, I cannot see the library, in the general sense, being reduced to a "small room" anytime soon, if ever. The real challenge facing libraries at the present time is finding ways to remain relevant in a world that does not necessarily have to rely upon the resources housed therein.

And it is at this point that we begin to see an apparent chasm open up between the needs of library patrons and the needs of the institutions created to serve them. Just about any competent library patron can over time be counted upon to develop the skills necessary to become an independent user with little need to consult the resident librarians or draw upon their expertise. But in the past, patrons still had to physically enter the library in order to retrieve books, and for this reason the library remained vital to their research. Many changes have taken place in a brief interval, however, and these days sources of electronic information can be accessed from any location, all that is needed being the proper equipment and a connection to a network service such as the World Wide Web. Librarians have been placed in the unaccustomed position of seeing their primary duty—the provision of information—taken out of their hands, of seeing their patrons prosper without their assistance. Librarians everywhere are struggling to come to terms with the fact that many kinds of advanced research can be performed by scholars in the comfort of their own homes and offices.

Is there any justification, then, in continuing to ask information seekers to venture into the library when the information they want is available elsewhere? Does the survival of the library as a functioning institution come before the needs of patrons?

As with many technological advancements leading to changes in social structures, the central question surrounding electronic textual information and the role it will play in our future is one of degree. Most information being generated these days is available in electronic form. But we should ask ourselves, Is that all anyone needs? And does the simple fact that it is available electronically make it more valuable or relevant to scholars conducting research than information available only in printed form? The truth is that we are not about to turn our backs on the past. There has been too much time and money and emotional capital invested in the technology of print on paper for it to be rendered obsolete, even in the long term. And this is true of printed work in all subject areas, not just the humanities. Those who hope to conduct research projects using only electronic sources will soon discover they are only scratching the surface, that there is a wealth of material eluding their grasp. The truest test of relevance and validity for most writing is not whether it is available in electronic form but whether other writers make use of it. Works that have been frequently cited by writers working in the same field of study are likely to still be relevant, even after many years. The actual form in which these works exist—manuscript, print, microform, electronic—is immaterial. If they continue to be consulted, then they can be considered current. Libraries will continue to fulfill a necessary role for scholars because they house materials that are only available as tangible objects. And regardless of whether they prefer a purely electronic environment or not, scholars will require these materials for their research.

Despite some dire prognostications, then, it is very likely that libraries will continue to play a role in our education. If we accept that one reason for the existence of the library as we know it is to store written materials and provide access to them, then it is a simple matter to extend this function to include electronic material, even if the library is only one of many places where it can be "found." As well, the best place to learn *how* to find information, regardless of format, has always been the library. Libraries will continue to fulfil this role in the electronic environment as they did in the print environment. The teaching function will remain, even if other aspects of librarianship disappear.

But there is no denying that electronic technologies have made forward strides—whether or not one regards this as "progress" is a subject for another debate—and the fact is that library administrators have no choice but to acquire electronic materials if they wish their collections to remain current and useful. The issue has been raised before, and discussed at length, but it is worth repeating that some sources of textual information, such as research papers and journals, are *only* available in electronic form. Also, the increasingly prohibitive costs associated with some paper products, again such as journals, means that in order to continue providing access to these items at all, libraries will have to begin subscribing to them in their electronic form. Scarcity of funds has already provided a great impetus to the creation of electronic journals and texts—which in the non-commercial setting are much cheaper to produce and deliver than their paper counterparts—and will likely play an important role as well in the ultimate success of these publications as libraries face reduced budgets and are compelled to seek alternative means of enlarging their collections and meeting the demands of patrons.

> Once many journals become available electronically, paper copies are likely to disappear. It will be a case of positive feedback operating in a destructive mode. Necessary information will be available electronically, and most of it will have to be accessed electronically, since the local libraries will not be able to provide copies of all relevant journals. (Odlyzko)

But how are libraries to actually go about collecting, storing, and providing access to electronic materials? One scenario has libraries filled, not with books, but with row upon row of computer terminals, each wired to the network, ready and waiting for the patron in need of electronic products to arrive. However, it is not likely that libraries will squander limited resources in such an extravagant manner. More probable (both in times of fiscal restraint and in the short term) is an "on-demand" service, in which the library's role is to retrieve the required document from the remote site and either let the patron read it on the screen or else print it out or deliver it to the patron electronically. This type of service resembles the conventional computer search and falls naturally within the mandate of existing document delivery departments. There would be little in the way of restructuring or adaptation required of the library.

Any service of this nature would of course rely heavily upon communication links, and as well upon the continuing viability of the remote sites producing and housing the electronic texts. In order to successfully implement this aspect of the "virtual library" some reliance on external mechanisms and institutions must be assumed.

> The most fundamental precept of the virtual library is the universal application of advanced high-speed computing and telecommunications capabilities to the access and delivery of information resources. Carried to its ultimate end, the virtual library offers a universe of information to any user, anywhere in the world, at any time of the day or night through the power of a personal computer with telecommunication capabilities. (Rooks 22)

In order for libraries to participate in this new universe, the first notion that we should consider abandoning is the one that equates access with bibliographic control and requires that documents fall under the jurisdiction of a library. This is not to say that we must forego the well-established practice of resource-sharing among libraries. The primary difference between this new arrangement and past practice is that the archival function has been transferred from the library to the publisher or supplier. This seemingly unavoidable circumstance could have serious ramifications on library policies and budgets, especially if suppliers decide to take advantage of consumer dependence and begin charging for access in the same way that producers of online databases charge hourly rates for searching privileges.

> A key issue is the state of libraries' readiness and willingness to archive electronic journals. On the one hand, librarians have little desire to become computer center managers. On the other hand they understand that if they only licence access to information that is owned by a publisher then their role as librarian is diminished. They become little more than a conduit to the publisher for university funds. For a library to own electronic materials it must archive them. This in turn requires computing facilities and new expertise. (Franks, "What is...")

As many of us can readily attest, libraries have been paying a substantial price for journal subscriptions for many years. And in these opportunistic times, it seems naïve to expect this to change simply because journals are being made available in a new and cheaper format. But even if this *does* happen—even if prices take a significant plunge— the chief problems remain those of access and control. I suspect that the solution proposed by John Franks—that libraries acquire extensive computing facilities in order to archive electronic journals—is not a feasible option in most cases. But until all libraries assume some means of local control, librarians have to accept that they will be waiting for communication networks to acquire a much higher degree of stability than most of these systems currently exhibit—something that may never happen, though fibre optic technology holds out some promise—before they can guarantee the immediate availability of everything in the electronic arena. Some may argue that librarians cannot even guarantee that a specific book will actually be found on the shelf in the place where the online or card catalogue says it is, and this is of course true. However, the difference is that the catalogue assures the patron that, though it may be momentarily inaccessible, a particular item is in fact part of the library collection. The electronic network offers no such assurances. And even if libraries begin storing electronic materials on site, cataloguing them and assigning them subject headings and call numbers, there will always remain a mechanized intermediary between the user and the electronic text, a machine that can "crash" or go "down" or become infected with a virus, a piece of equipment that will always be vulnerable to any number of extraneous phenomena that can undermine control and interfere with access.

It is a common refrain found in much of the literature on the future of librarianship that librarians are in danger of becoming obsolete and that, in these times of electronic ascendancy, we should all be striving to re-create ourselves as "information professionals."

The assumption is that the "virtual library" is just around the corner and that if we allow ourselves to stagnate in print mode, our role as information providers will be assumed by an entirely different community of information sleuths who are willing to take risks and who are less bound by traditional methods. This kind of fatalism is routinely voiced whenever technological change appears to threaten the roles that people have fashioned for themselves and grown accustomed to over time, either as individuals or as professionals. Because electronic text combined with communication technology seems to threaten the library as a "place" where one can go to find "things," we hear the death knell sounded for the library and the librarian as we have come to know them. This has given rise to a body of writing, some of which has been quoted here, that envisages libraries in varying degrees of dismemberment, their collections and staffing complements depleted and replaced by machines, their functions appropriated by a variety of commercial enterprises in the business of providing information for a fee.

I oppose this view, as much because it allows for no compromise as for the fact that technological change does not move at the same rate all over the world. Is it reasonable to expect the library as a place to be swallowed up in the rush toward some electronic utopia? Are we moving forward so rapidly that a networked computer terminal and a CD-ROM or two are all we need for the cultivation of our senses and the nurture of our minds? I have hardly even touched upon the importance of libraries and their contents to children, but I have seen scant evidence to suggest that children's books, with their colourful and detailed illustrations and large print, will make a convincing transfer to the computer screen. Neither will many of us willingly relinquish our own public libraries, a learning space that opens a world of discovery, helps us develop lifelong interests and in many cases has assisted in fashioning the very individuals we have become. Some of us simply enjoy being in the library, we appreciate the physical space, the civilized atmosphere of learning that invites us to explore. It is an emotional connection to a place and to a part of ourselves. As William Birdsall observes in *The Myth of the Electronic Library*, "A sense of place is existential. It is a combination of sacred and profane, perceptual and geographical, natural and built, cognitive and emotional." And further along, "The library as place has nurtured generations of users through an appeal to sentient feelings of loyalty, affection, safety, excitement, and awe" (65).

As well, the role of the librarian has always been more complex than simply that of the "information provider." Librarians do much more than answer questions, something even a monkey can do if the question is posed in the right way. Librarians could be more correctly described as "knowledge brokers" and knowledge is very different from information. Traditionally, it is the primary concern of the public service librarian that all patrons who enter the library learn how to use the resources housed there to the fullest extent possible. And this involves interacting with people, discovering what their needs are, and finding a way to fill those needs as thoroughly as available resources allow. The teaching and nurturing aspects of librarianship are often overlooked. One hopes that after interacting with librarians working in a professional capacity, individuals will possess more knowledge than previously and perhaps even a better understanding of the questions they need to ask. To many people whose contact with them is occasional and casual, information technologies—both print and electronic—can be mysterious, perplexing, and somewhat intimidating. The librarian's role is to demystify these technologies and to enhance the learning process; in other words, to teach people how to learn and perhaps even to instill a desire to learn. This is not something that can take place in the "virtual library."

Despite these sentiments, however, the proliferation of electronic text means that some measure of control will be lost and that librarians have to take a lead role in developing ways to organize electronic text. Access to the Internet does not constitute ownership or control. At present, the site where a certain text originates is under no obligation to maintain that text or even to continue to make it available. Unless electronic materials are printed out on paper or downloaded to disk, and then catalogued and assigned call numbers and locations, they do not become part of the local library collection. This is unavoidable. Nor are patrons compelled to access them in the traditional manner, that is, by coming into the library.

> The advent of the virtual library will effect a major transition in how we deliver library services. We can no longer expect users to be present in the library to ask for assistance or to be available for traditional library instruction. The delivery of services to a primarily remote group of users through a networked system will mandate a fresh look at how libraries are organized, staffed, and funded to deliver services and information. (Rooks 25)

It is hardly out of the question that in the future some form of the "virtual library" may enter into practice. Still, it seems unlikely that it will entirely replace the existing library, with its browsable book stacks and human interface and primitive study tables and reference desk. More likely is a model that combines the two, a library that provides facilities for print-based research in close proximity to networked computer terminals where patrons can connect with World Wide Web sites and retrieve electronic documents either from the library's collection or from the far side of the globe and where librarians can field questions from people who may prefer to work at home or who may live hundreds of miles away.

Collective Memory

The progression from oral to literate culture diminished the capacity of our minds to store information while making possible an expanded body of knowledge. As more and more people took advantage of emerging writing technologies to set their theories and findings down on paper, what was out there to be known (as opposed to what was absolutely essential to know for the sake of survival) quickly grew beyond the capacity of any single individual to ever learn let alone memorize. The ascendancy of the convenient and compact book as the information storage medium of choice made possible the institution that has become our modern library—with its miles of shelves and intricate means of recording and cataloguing current holdings. Libraries have become our storehouses of culture, visibly symbolic of humanity's ability to create worlds with texts and to forge new knowledge out of old. I have argued that each new written work makes either explicit or implicit reference to works that preceded it, and this would not have been possible without the preserved written record of previous cultures, the culture of last week and the culture of six hundred years ago. The function of the library has been to store these records, to maintain them, and to ensure their availability for years to come. Our own memory capacity is much too limited, and so we rely upon the library to remember for us, in the collective sense, like an enormous brain packed with knowledge from which we can retrieve what we want whenever the need arises. It is true that without libraries we would know only what we could store within our minds and within our immediate living spaces. To the individual unable to locate it, all other information would be as good as lost. We would stagnate, "reinventing the wheel" at every turn.

There is concern that the widespread acceptance and application of electronic text will impair this process of collective memorization, which is in fact a process of preservation. For knowledge to endure it has to be permanently recorded, but questions persist about the permanence of electronic text, which in some circles is still regarded as ephemeral and essentially unstable, hardly a worthy successor to print, though perhaps a necessary one. Electronic text is vulnerable in ways that print is not, vulnerable to the idiosyncratic nature of the machine, the availability of continual sources of power, the reliability of back-up mechanisms, the compatibility of software and hardware, the level of expertise of the person trying to access the text and read it. A book can be misplaced or stolen, but in many cases can be recovered or repurchased; when electronic text is lost it is often lost for good.

Furthermore, information stored in electronic form is not always accessible in the same democratic fashion and to the same clientele as print. Hidden within the machine, or at the other end of an invisible network, it requires special knowledge of those who wish to obtain it, knowledge that does not belong to everyone in equal measure. It is true that knowledge of books is not equally distributed either. But libraries exist to make this kind of knowledge universally available and easily accessible. But because electronic text requires a rather specialized type of knowledge as well as expensive equipment, it is unlikely to begin making a profound difference in everyone's life anytime soon. Unlike the information and entertainment provided by television—a truly democratic medium that requires very little of anybody—electronic text has so far fallen somewhat short of achieving universal appeal, of demonstrating its viability outside of the rather elitist realms of scholarship and business. It is not yet widely perceived as an end in itself. Rather, it is regarded as a rather arcane tool which facilitates a process, the final result of which is text printed on paper.

Electronic text moves faster than print and is much more flexible, yet there are limits to what it can do and to the amount and variety of information it can convey. In the field of literary studies, a great deal of serious attention is devoted to original manuscripts and correspondence. Creative writers normally progress through a series of drafts before presenting the final version of a work to a publisher, and these drafts bear markings made by the authors themselves, scribbled instructions for editors and typesetters. This can still occur to a certain extent, if the author chooses to print a draft of the work-in-progress and annotate it by hand. However, as we have seen, word processing has made editing less of a burden by eliminating the need for hard copy at every editorial stage. Changes can be made directly on the screen. No printed copy need be produced at all. As this saves paper, and therefore trees, it is a boon for the environment. But what we lose are the interim versions of what could well become our future classic works, and not just of literature, but of social, historical, political, and scientific scholarship as well. The same holds true for original correspondence, which is often where authors are most candid and open about their own works and the works of others, and about the creative process. There have been writers, such as Virginia Woolf, whose correspondence on its own forms a rich body of work. Scholars are therefore justified in their concern

> about the preservation of authors' and composers' original manuscripts. The marks and corrections on paper documents can give scholars a deep insight into the artist's original intentions. Is the scholarly exchange by email an electronic equivalent? (Ryan, Goodacre, and Bittinger)

It is true that Shakespeare and many of his contemporaries did not regard their working drafts or correspondence as important and so took no measures to preserve them. This is a permanent loss to scholarship. But the intervening centuries have seen a shift in values, and authors everywhere have been saving their papers at the behest of scholars and archivists. It is quite conceivable, however, that in years to come trace evidence of the evolutionary process through which works of literature and scholarship pass on their way to completion will no longer be preserved. Can there be any doubt that this will hamper studies in all disciplines and make certain kinds of intensive research impossible?

For many, the computer is still a rather arcane and forbidding entity. This is nobody's fault. But the fact of the matter is that the mechanical interface stands as a barrier to knowledge and learning, and ultimately, to memory. Most people feel they have a choice, and many still choose to write their poems and stories (or recipes or Christmas cards) by hand, to scribble annotations in the margins of books using a pencil, to jot down their daily impressions in private notebooks using their favourite pen. There are people who will choose not to perform a certain task if it involves becoming acquainted with computerized systems. Certainly, this is not an attitude that should be promoted or encouraged. We should all be as open as possible to the idea of acquiring knowledge regardless of its format and regardless of the interface. However, saying this should be the case does not actually make it the case. People have a right to choose. Providing information only in electronic form literally excludes a certain portion of society from ever accessing it, because they lack either the means or the will. And even though people are still making choices, this is a form of censorship because it is the medium of information exchange, not the content of that exchange, which is forcing a certain choice on them.

The aim of those who labour to develop new information technologies is, of course, to build rather than to destroy, to enhance rather than to inhibit. As time goes on, electronic text and the machinery associated with it are likely to become more pervasive rather than less, and so we can expect most if not all the deficiencies of this format to which I have referred to eventually be addressed. The technology itself will certainly become more reliable and more generally available, and once this has occurred the concept of electronic text will penetrate more deeply into the collective public consciousness. As the generations raised on print culture age, and their preferences, biases, and assumptions recede into the past, electronic text will become established as a valuable entity in its own right, existing apart from print and no longer subject to comparisons. As with any new and successful technology, electronic text is gradually being absorbed into the mainstream of popular culture. It may or may not totally supersede the book, but in either case it will continue to transform how we approach, access, absorb, and recall information.

5

The Future

Today, there are more people writing more words than at any other time in human history. Thousands of books are published every year. Newspapers, magazines, and journals proliferate in both paper and electronic formats. Is there any point in even trying to keep up with this lavish output?

The fact is that we cannot keep up and probably never have. Machines have made writing a simple and effortless activity, and have made the transfer of text from one location to another a matter of one or two keystrokes. As people become accustomed to the technology, a greater number either wish or feel compelled to take part, and it is becoming easier than ever for them to do so. Already the sum total of human knowledge grows each day and expands exponentially over the course of any given year. There are of course limits to what any single library can acquire, but taken collectively the holdings of all libraries make available everything that is out there to be known. Apart from the fact that we can never hope to make use of it in one lifetime, the question remains, do we really need all that information?

We already know that it is not solely a question of need, or even of demand. There is writing being produced today that may not appear relevant, or important, or even entirely rational for generations. This has often been the case in the past, before the establishment of formal mechanisms for storage and retrieval, when the preservation of almost all writing was overwhelmingly a matter of chance. We can only imagine how many valuable works of literature, of scholarship, of theory, were irretrievably lost down through the ages because unique copies were destroyed, either deliberately or by accident. Indeed, we should count ourselves fortunate that we live at a time when there exists a variety of methods to produce, duplicate, store, and disseminate our written works.

Certain parts of the world are destined to lag behind others as far as technological progress is concerned, and in these less advanced regions print will likely continue to serve the purpose quite adequately for years to come. We should not therefore be so hasty to proclaim the demise of a technology that has served us in exemplary fashion for hundreds of years and which will in all likelihood persist as a viable option for writers long after those with their sanguinary predictions have passed into obscurity.

My own feeling is that the rate of transition from print to electronic dominance will be governed by factors that may seem extraneous to the present discussion, economic and ecological factors over which we will have little control. If we consider that paper is the product of an environment almost universally under seige, that raw materials are dwindling with little concern for replenishment in circles of power, that the process of manufacture is becoming more costly each year, we arrive inevitably at the conclusion that electronic text may win out by default on the very day that paper becomes a scarce and prohibitively expensive commodity. We have seen subscription prices for scholarly journals take excessive leaps on an annual basis for many years, to the point where libraries serving specific regions have begun to coordinate their collection policies as a means of defence. As well, book prices continue to climb at a pace well beyond the rate of inflation. These developments can only go on for so long before a threshold is reached, at which point print on paper will no longer be perceived as the most reasonable or efficient way to preserve words or to move information from one place to another.

And where do writers fit into the technological scheme of things? Generalizations are difficult, but there is no reason to doubt that the act of writing will persist, that the creative urge will continue to manifest itself throughout the coming years. When we glance back into the past, we see that writers have always regarded their task in the same way even when new technologies introduced new ways of doing things and asked that they perform their labours, for instance, on a keyboard rather than with a pen. Writers, like other people engaged in less exotic activities, adapt quite well to change. And if for some reason the current generation resists what the more powerful computers have to offer, then it will fall to the next generation to face the challenge and derive the benefits. And there will always be a next generation. However, some people will want to cling to antiquated or outmoded ways of doing things, and it is probably wise to keep in mind that this does not make their work any more or less artistically sound than someone who stood in line in the rain waiting to buy the first copy of Windows '95. The calibre of the work will continue to reflect the quality of the writer's mind, not the quality of his or her equipment or software.

Writers are not about to give up and become bus drivers just because the final product appears in electronic rather than paper form either. The reasons for writing have always existed apart from the form the writing ultimately takes, and this will not change. Many people write and never see their work published. The fundamental need to give expression to an inner voice, and to explore language and exploit its potentials, provide the impetus to continue writing, even when the work is ignored. What *will* change radically in years to come is the writing process itself. New technologies are evolving all the time. Writers may soon find that they do not even need a pen or a keyboard in order to set their ideas down once voice-activated word processors pass through the development stages and hit the open market. Who would waste their time and effort "writing" when a machine can translate dictation directly into electronic text? After all, a hundred years ago Henry James dictated many of his greatest works to a private secretary. Perhaps if we were free of the burdensome task of actually putting pen to paper writing would come more easily and creativity would flourish. With a little help we could all be Henry James.

This is speculation, and somewhat playful speculation at that. The fact of the matter is that directions in technological innovation, like the profusion of other forces that affect our lives, cannot be predicted with any degree of accuracy.

It will be many years before the collected works of humankind in printed form find their way into machine-readable form. Likewise, it will be many years before all writers without exception begin and end every work on a computer. Perhaps the day will come. Perhaps not. But it will only be on that momentous day that someone somewhere will be able to declare print to be dead. Whether or not you believe the benefits of such an outcome will outweigh the costs depends entirely upon your point of view and your own personal convictions concerning print and technology. However, we, from our humble vantage point of the present day, can say whatever we like. We can make forecasts and issue warnings and even stamp our feet in protest. It is still very likely that the determining factors will be forces over which we will have little or no control.

If the time ever comes for print and handwriting to be relegated to the museum, we can certainly hope that practising writers are permitted input into the decision process. And if they decide to carry on their activities in an electronic rather than print-based medium, they will simply be taking advantage of technology to make their working lives easier, something we all do without thinking and without apology, which is as it should be.

Bibliography

Most of the sources I've consulted in the preparation of this volume are, ironically enough, taken from conventional books and journals. The citations for these items are complete. I have also made use of a number of electronic sources, such as articles from electronic journals, papers that exist as electronic preprints or drafts on the Internet, and private e-mail. Except in the rarest of cases these items are not formatted to make use of page numbers. I have therefore not used page numbers in citations for these items.

I have followed MLA style throughout, using the 4th edition of the *MLA Handbook for Writers of Research Papers* (1995), prepared by Joseph Gibaldi.

Alkalay-Gut, Karen. "My Friend the Computer." E-mail to the author. 1 June 1994.

Amiran, Eyal, and John Unsworth. "*Postmodern Culture*: Publishing in the Electronic Medium." *The Public-Access Computer Systems Review* 2.1 (1991): 67-76. Online. Internet. March 1994. Available gopher://vm.utcc.utoronto.ca:70/00/pacsrev/pacsv2/amiran.prv2n1.

Amiran, Eyal, Elaine Orr, and John Unsworth. "Refereed Electronic Journals and the Future of Scholarly Publishing." *Advances in Library Automation and Networking: a Research Annual* 4 (1991): 25-53.

Arms, William Y. "Scholarly Publishing on the National Networks." *Scholarly Publishing* 23.3 (1992): 158-69.

Bailey, Charles W., Jr. "Electronic (Online) Publishing in Action: *The Public-Access Computer Systems Review* and other Electronic Serials." *Online* 15.1 (1991): 28-35.

---. "Libraries with Glass Walls." *The Public-Access Computer Systems Review* 1.2 (1990): 91-93. Online. Internet. March 1994. Available gopher://vm.utcc.utoronto.ca:70/00/pacsrev/pacsv1/bailey.prv1n2.

Ballentine, Karen. "Re: Feedback requested on electronic writing." E-mail to the author. 6 June 1994.

Barthes, Roland. "The Death of the Author." *The Rustle of Language*. Trans. Richard Howard. New York: Hill and Wang, 1986. 49-55.

Basch, Reva. "Books Online: Visions, Plans, and Perspectives for Electronic Text." *Online* 15.4 (1991): 13-23.

Birdsall, William F. *The Myth of the Electronic Library: Librarianship and Social Change in America*. Westport, Conn.: Greenwood Press, 1994.

Birkerts, Sven. *The Gutenberg Elegies: The Fate of Reading in an Electronic Age*. Boston: Faber & Faber, 1994.

Bolter, Jay David. *Writing Space: the Computer, Hypertext, and the History of Writing.* Hillsdale, N.J.: L. Erlbaum, 1991.

Brent, Doug. "Oral Knowledge, Typographical Knowledge, Electronic Knowledge: Speculations on the History of Ownership." *EJournal* 1.3 (1991). Online. Internet. March 1994. Available gopher://gopher.acs.ohio-state.edu/Journals & Newsletters/ OSU Libraries' Electronic Serials/EJournal/ejrnlv1.n3.

Burke, James. *The Day the Universe Changed.* London: British Broadcasting Corporation, 1985.

Burnett, Kathleen. "The Scholar's Rhizome: Networked Communication Issues." *The Arachnet Electronic Journal on Virtual Culture* 1.2 (1993). Online. Internet. March 1994. Available gopher://gopher.usask.ca/Library/E-journals/Humanities & Social Sciences/The Arachnet Electronic Journal on Virtual Culture/1993 v.1/ Arachnet Electronic Journal on Virtual Culture, v 1 n 2 - April.

—. "Toward a Theory of Hypertextual Design." *Postmodern Culture* 3.2 (1993). Online. Internet. March 1994. Available http://jefferson.village.virginia.edu/pmc/ issue.193/burnett.193.

Cassidy, Paul. "Re: Feedback requested on electronic writing." E-mail to the author. 1 June 1994.

Chappell, Warren. *A Short History of the Printed Word.* New York: Knopf, 1970.

Clanchy, M. T. *From Memory to Written Record: England 1066-1307.* 2nd ed. Oxford: Blackwell, 1993.

Coniam, David. "Literacy for the Next Generation: Writing Without Handwriting." *EJournal* 2.2 (1992). Online. Internet. March 1994. Available gopher:// gopher.acs.ohio-state.edu/Journals & Newsletters/OSU Libraries' Electronic Serials/EJournal/ejrnlv2.n2.

Cortázar, Julio. *Hopscotch.* Trans. Gregory Rabassa. New York: Pantheon Books, 1966.

Crawford, Walt, and Michael Gorman. *Future Libraries: Dreams, Madness, & Reality.* Chicago: American Library Association, 1995.

Crocker, Steve. "The Political and Social Implications of the Net." Unpublished essay, 1992. Online. Internet. March 1994. Available e-mail: aq817@Cleveland.freenet.edu.

Crump, Eric. "Writing on/with/in a computer." E-mail to the author. 1 June 1994.

—. "Welcome message for CREWRT-L." E-mail to the author. 15 June 1994.

Douglas, J. Yellowlees. "'How do I stop this thing?': Closure and Indeterminacy in Interactive Narratives." *Hyper/Text/Theory.* Ed. George Landow. Baltimore: Johns Hopkins University Press, 1994. 159-88.

Eisenberg, Daniel. "The Electronic Journal." *Scholarly Publishing* 20.1 (1988): 49-58.

Eisenstein, Elizabeth L. *The Printing Press as an Agent of Change: Communications and Cultural Transformations in Early-Modern Europe*. Cambridge: Cambridge University Press, 1979.

Elmer-Dewitt, Philip. "First Nation in Cyberspace." *Time* 142.24 (6 December 1993): 44-46.

Febvre, Lucien, and Henri-Jean Martin. *The Coming of the Book: The Impact of Printing, 1450-1800*. Trans. David Gerard. Ed. Geoffrey Nowell-Smith and David Wootton. London: NLB, 1976.

Foucault, Michel. "What is an Author?" *Language, Counter-Memory, Practice: Selected Essays and Interviews*. Ed. Donald F. Bouchard. Trans. Donald F. Bouchard and Sherry Simon. Ithaca, N.Y.: Cornell University Press, 1977. 113-38.

Franks, John. "The Impact of Electronic Publication on Scholarly Journals." *Notices of the American Mathematical Society* 40.9 (1993): 1200-2.

—. "What is an Electronic Journal?" Online. Internet. March 1994. Available gopher:/ /gopher.cic.net:2000/00/e-serials/About_Electronic_Publishing/what-is-ejournal-1,-2,-3,-4.

Ghiselin, Brewster, ed. *The Creative Process: A Symposium*. New York: New American Library, 1952.

Goody, Jack. *The Interface Between the Written and the Oral*. Cambridge: Cambridge University Press, 1987.

Goodyear, Mary Lou. "Information Policy for Electronic Information Sources." *The Public-Access Computer Systems Review* 4.6 (1993): 23-31. Online. Internet. March 1994. Available gopher://gopher.acs.ohio-state.edu/0/Journals & Newsletters/ OSU Libraries' Electronic Serials/Public-Access Comp. Sys. Review/pacrv4n6/ goodyear

Guédon, Jean-Claude. "Electronic Journals: The Way of the Future?" *Bulletin* (The Canadian Federation for the Humanities) 16.1 & 2 (1993): 3-6.

Hane, Paula. "Paper: The Security Blanket of the Electronic Age." *Database* 14.1 (1991): 6-7.

Harnad, Stevan. "Implementing Peer Review on the Net: Scientific Quality Control in Scholarly Electronic Journals." Online. Internet. March 1994. Available ftp:// ftp.princeton.edu/pub/harnad/Harnad/harnad95.peer.review.

—. "Interactive Publication: Extending the American Physical Society's discipline-specific model for electronic publishing." *Serials Review* 18.1/2 (1992): 58-61.

—. "Post-Gutenberg Galaxy: The Fourth Revolution in the Means of Production of Knowledge." *The Public-Access Computer Systems Review* 2.1 (1991): 39-53. Online. Internet. March 1994. Available gopher://vm.utcc.utoronto.ca:70/00/pacsrev/ pacsv2/harnad.prv2n1.

—. "Scholarly Skywriting and the Prepublication Continuum of Scientific Inquiry." *Psychological Science* 1.6 (1990): 342-44.

Harrison, Teresa M., Timothy Stephen, and James Winter. "Online Journals: Disciplinary Designs for Electronic Scholarship." *The Public-Access Computer Systems Review* 2.1 (1991): 25-38. Online. Internet. March 1994. Available gopher://vm.utcc.utoronto.ca:70/00/pacsrev/pacsv2/harrison.prv2n1.

Hart, Michael. "Project Gutenberg: Access to Electronic Texts." *Database* 13.6 (1990): 6-9.

Heim, Michael. *Electric Language: A Philosophical Study of Word Processing.* New Haven: Yale University Press, 1987.

Hoke, Franklin. "Publication by Internet." *The Scientist* 8.9 (May 2, 1994): 8.

Holland, Norman N. "Eliza Meets the Postmodern." *EJournal* 4.1 (1994). Online. Internet. April 1994. Available gopher://gopher.acs.ohio-state.edu/Journals & Newsletters/OSU Libraries' Electronic Serials/EJournal/ejrnlv4.n1.

Holt-Fortin, Cher. "Re: Feedback requested on electronic writing." E-mail to the author. 1 June 1994.

Howard, Teresa L. "Feedback—Electronic Writing." E-mail to the author. 6 June 1994.

Johnson, Elmer D. *Communication: An Introduction to the History of Writing, Printing, Books, and Libraries.* 4th ed. Metuchan, N.J.: Scarecrow Press, 1973.

Joyce, Michael. "Notes Toward an Unwritten Non-linear Electronic Text: The Ends of Print Culture (a work in progress)." *Postmodern Culture* 2.1 (1991): 45 pars. Online. Internet. March 1994. Available http://jefferson.village.virginia.edu/pmc/issue.991/joyce.991.

—. *Of Two Minds: Hypertext Pedagogy and Poetics.* Ann Arbor: University of Michigan Press, 1995.

Kantrowitz, Barbara. "Men, Women, & Computers." *Newsweek* (16 May 1994): 48-55.

Katzen, May. "Electronic Publishing in the Humanities." *Scholarly Publishing* 18.1 (1986): 5-16.

Klemperer, Katharina. "Electronic Texts: Introduction." *Information Technology and Libraries* 13.1 (1994): 6.

Landow, George P. *Hypertext: the Convergence of Contemporary Critical Theory and Technology.* Baltimore: Johns Hopkins University Press, 1992.

—. "What's a Critic to Do?: Critical Theory in the Age of Hypertext." *Hyper/Text/Theory.* Ed. George Landow. Baltimore: Johns Hopkins University Press, 1994. 1-48.

Lanham, Richard A. *The Electronic Word: Democracy, Technology, and the Arts.* Chicago: University of Chicago Press, 1993.

Lindsay, Robert K. "Electronic Journals of Proposed Research." *EJournal* 1.1 (1991). Online. Internet. March 1994. Available gopher://gopher.acs.ohio-state.edu/ Journals & Newsletters/OSU Libraries' Electronic Serials/EJournal/ejrnlv1.n1.

Maddox, Tom. "Reports From the Electronic Frontier: I Sing the Text Electric." Unpublished Paper, 1992. Online. Internet. February 1994. Available gopher:// gopher.well.sf.ca.us:70/0/Publications/LOCUS/reports.3.

Maule, R. William. "Infrastructure Issues in Computer-related Communication." *Electronic Journal of Communication* 3.2 (1993). Available e-mail: send request "Send Maule V3N293" to Comserve@vm.its.rpi.edu.

McKinney, Brian. "Writing Vs. Typing" Online posting. Listserv CREWRT-L@MIZZOU1.BITNET. 20 June 1994.

McKnight, Cliff, Andrew Dillon, and John Richardson. *Hypertext in Context.* Cambridge: Cambridge University Press, 1991.

McLuhan, Marshall. *The Gutenberg Galaxy: The Making of Typographic Man.* Toronto: University of Toronto Press, 1962.

Miller, Karl. *Authors.* Oxford: Clarendon Press, 1989.

Negroponte, Nicholas. *Being Digital.* New York: Knopf, 1995.

Nielsen, Jakob. *Hypertext and Hypermedia.* Boston: Academic Press, 1990.

Nisonger, Thomas E. "Electronic Journals: Post-modern Dream or Nightmare: Report of the ALCTSCMDS Collection Development Librarians of Academic Libraries Discussion Group." *Library Acquisition: Practice and Theory* 17.3 (1993): 378-80.

Odlyzko, Andrew M. "Tragic Loss or Good Riddance? The Impending Demise of Traditional Scholarly Journals (preliminary version, 30 December 1993)." Online. Internet. Version of 6 November 1994 Available ftp://netlib.att.com/netlib/att/ math/odlyzko/index.html.

Okerson, Ann. "The Electronic Journal: What, Whence, and When?" *The Public-Access Computer Systems Review* 2.1 (1991): 5-24. Online. Internet. March 1994. Available gopher://vm.utcc.utoronto.ca/pacsrev/pacsv2/okerson.prv2n1.

Olsen, W. Scott. "A Mythic Sense of Place in the Electronic Community." Included in online posting "Stuff about us, I think." Listserv CREWRT-L@MIZZOU1.BITNET. 10 May 1994.

Ong, Walter J. *Orality and Literacy: the Technologizing of the Word.* London: Methuen, 1982.

Plato. *Plato's Phaedrus.* Trans. R. Hackforth. Cambridge: Cambridge University Press, 1952.

Quinn, Frank. "Roadkill on the Electronic Highway?: The Threat to the Mathematical Literature." Unpublished Essay, 1993. Online. Internet. January 1994. Available ftp://calvin.math.vt/edu/pub/quinn/roadkill.txt.

—. "A Role for Libraries in Electronic Publication." Unpublished Essay, 1992. Online. Internet. January 1994. Available ftp://calvin.math.vt/edu/pub/quinn/libraryRole.txt.

Rawlins, Gregory J. E. "The New Publishing: Technology's Impact on the Publishing Industry over the next Decade." *The Public-Access Computer Systems Review* 3.8 (1992): 5-63. Online. Internet. March 1994. Available gopher://vm.utcc.utoronto.ca:70/00/pacsrev/pacsv3/rawlins1.prv3n8 and rawlins2.prv3n8.

Rooks, Dana. "The Virtual Library: Pitfalls, Promises, and Potential." *The Public-Access Computer Systems Review* 4.5 (1993): 22-29. Online. Internet. March 1994. Available gopher://gopher.acs.ohio-state.edu/0/Journals & Newsletters/OSU Libraries' Electronic Serials/Public Access Comp. Sys. Review/pacrv4n5/rooks.

Ryan, Tony, Christine Goodacre, and Steven Bittinger. "Electronic Publishing." Online. Internet. March 1994. Available e-mail: Tony.Ryan@its.utas.edu.au.

Sader, Jennifer. "Re: Feedback requested on electronic writing." E-mail to the author. 1 June 1994.

Sewell, David. "The USENET Oracle: Virtual Authors and Network Community." *EJournal* 2.5 (1992). Online. Internet. March 1994. Available gopher://gopher.acs.ohio-state.edu/Journals & Newsletters/OSU Libraries' Electronic Serials/EJournal/ejrnlv2.n5.

Smith, Anthony. *Goodbye Gutenberg: The Newspaper Revolution of the 1980's*. New York: Oxford University Press, 1980.

Standera, O. L. "Electronic Publishing: Some Notes on Reader Response and Costs." *Scholarly Publishing* 16.4 (1985): 291-305.

Tuman, Myron C., ed. *Literacy Online: The Promise (and Peril) of Reading and Writing with Computers*. Pittsburgh: University of Pittsburgh Press, 1992.

Turoff, Murray and Starr Roxanne Hiltz. "The Electronic Journal: A Progress Report." *Journal of the American Society for Information Science* 33.4 (1982): 195-202.

Vansina, Jan. *Oral Tradition: A Study in Historical Methodology*. Trans. H.M. Wright. London: Routledge & Kegan Paul, 1965.

Biography

Ian Colford has a masters degree in English and an MLS, both from Dalhousie University. His short stories have appeared in a number of journals, including *Event* and *University Avenues*, and will appear shortly in *Grain*. He is presently employed in Social Sciences & Humanities Services in the Killam Library at Dalhousie University and is the editor of the *Pottersfield Portfolio*. He lives in Halifax with his wife Collette.

DALHOUSIE UNIVERSITY
SCHOOL OF LIBRARY AND INFORMATION STUDIES
OCCASIONAL PAPERS SERIES

(Prices listed do not include G.S.T.)

Series Editor: Bertrum H. MacDonald

---

8. *The Society for the Diffusion of Useful Knowledge, 1826-1864: A Social and Bibliographic Evaluation*, by Harold Smith. 1974. ISBN 0-7703-0145-2 $10.00.

9. *Developing Public Libraries in Canada from 1535-1983*, by Elizabeth Homer Morton. 1975. The Alberta Letts Memorial Lecture (All proceeds will be donated to the Alberta Letts Memorial Fellowship Fund.) ISBN 0-7703-0146-0 $6.00.

12. *The Helen F. MacRae Collection: A Bibliography of Korean Relations with Canadians and other Western Peoples which includes a Checklist of Documents and Reports 1898-1975*, compiled by Helen F. MacRae Parker Lee, edited by M. Doreen E. Fraser. 1976. ISSN 0318-7403 $10.00.

13. *The Information Needs of Physiotherapists with a Guide to Physiotherapy Collections for Community General Hospitals*, by M. Doreen E. Fraser and Hazel A. Lloyd. 2nd ed. 1981. ISBN 0-7703-0150-9 $9.00

15. *Access to Film Information: An Indexing and Retrieval System for the National Film Board of Canada*, by Mary Dykstra. 1977. ISBN 0-7703-0152-5 $15.00.

16. *A Guide to the Identification and Acquisition of Canadian Government Publications: Provinces and Territories*, by Catherine A. Pross. 2nd ed. 1983. ISBN 0-7703-0165-7 $11.50.

17. *The Development of Public Library Services in Newfoundland 1934-1972*, by Jessie Mifflen. 1978. ISBN 0-7703-0154-1 $10.00.

18. *Source Documents for American Bibliography: Three "McMurtrie Manuals,"* by Scott Bruntjen. 1978. ISBN 0-7703-0156-8 $10.00

19. *Canadian Plays—A Supplementary Checklist to 1945*, by Patrick B. O'Neill. 1978. ISBN 0-7703-0158-4 $10.00.

20. *Libraries and Popular Education: Proceedings of a One Day Symposium Held at the School of Library Service, Dalhousie University, March 31, 1978*, edited by Boris Raymond. 1978. ISBN 0-7703-9162-2 $10.00

21. *A Survey and Listing of Nova Scotia Newspapers, 1752-1957*, by Gertrude Tratt. 1979. ISBN 0-7703-0160-6 $11.50

24. *The Canadian School-Housed Public Library*, by L.J. Amey. 1979. ISBN 0-7703-0159-2 $16.50

27. *Perceptions of the High School Librarian*, by John Rainforth. 1981. ISBN 0-7703-0168-1 $11.50.

28. *The Conservation of Library Materials*, by Alice Harrison. 1981. ISBN 0-7703-0164-9 $14.50.

30. *The Development of the Department of Library Science, Ahmadu Bello University, Nigeria and its Implications for the Planning of Library Education Programmes in English-speaking Black African Countries*, by Edward Anthony Olden. (Master of Library Science thesis, Ahmadu Bello University). 1982. ISBN 0-7703-0170-3 $11.50.

31. *Libraries and the Law: Proceedings of the Atlantic Provinces Library Association Conference 1980, Held in Corner Brook, Newfoundland, May 1-4, 1980.* Publications Committee, Atlantic Provinces Library Association, edited by Heather Creech. 1983. ISBN 0-7703-0167-3 $11.50.

32. *Research and Information Science: What Where We've Been Says About Where We Are*, by Martha M. West. 1983. ISBN 0-7703-0175-4 $11.50.

33. *An Index to* Acadiensis *1901-1908*, by Dorothy Cooke. 1983. ISBN 0-7703-0171-1 $11.50.

34. *Urban Public Library Service for the Aging in Canada*, by Lois M. Bewley and Sylvia Crooks. 1984. ISBN 0-7703-0181-9 $14.50.

35. *Information, Enrichment and Delight: Public Libraries in Western Australia*, by John Cook. 1985. ISBN 0-7703-0176-2 $16.50.

36. *Canadian Poetry in Selected English-Language Anthologies: An Index and Guide*, edited by Margery Fee. 1985. ISBN 0-7703-0183-5 $21.95.

37. *The Introduction of Automated Library and Information Services in a Newly Industrialized Country: A Case Study of the Brazilian Experience*, by Cavan M. McCarthy. 1985. ISBN 0-7703-0169-X $16.50.

38. *A History of the Dublin Library Society 1791-1881*, by John Bruce Howell. 1985. ISBN 0-7703-0178-9 $11.50.

39. *PRECIS: Recent Applications*, edited by Mary Dykstra. 1986. ISBN 0-7703-0182-7 $14.50.

40. *Nova Scotia Variant Place Names*, by Dorothy L. Cooke. 1986. ISBN 0-7703-9710-7 $11.50.

41. *The Marigold System: A Case Study of Community Planning Networks and Community Development*, by Robin Inskip. 1987. ISBN 0-7703-9712-3 $14.50.

42. *Public Library Boards in Postwar Ontario, 1945-1985*, by Lorne Bruce and Karen Bruce. 1988. ISBN 0-7703-9716-6 $16.50.

43. *Literary Presses in Canada, 1975-1985: A Checklist and Bibliography*, compiled by Holly Melanson. 1988. ISBN 0-7703-9717-4 $16.50.

44. *Sustaining Earth: A Bibliography of the Holdings of the Ecology Action Resource Centre, Halifax, Canada*, compiled by Catherine Pross and Mary Dwyer-Rigby. 1988. ISBN 0-7703-9718-2 $18.00.

45. *Subject Access and Bibliographic Instruction: Two Sides of the OPAC Problem*, introduced by Mary Dykstra. 1988. ISBN 0-7720-9720-4 $12.50

46. *Libraries and Library Services in Portugal*, by Nell Buller. 1988. ISBN 0-7703-9722-0 $16.00.

47. *Canadian Poets: Vital Facts on English-writing Poets Born from 1730 through 1910*, by Arnold T. Schwab. 1989. ISBN 0-7703-9734-4 $17.50.

48. *Organizing a Research Agenda: Information Studies for the 1990s. Proceedings of a Symposium Held at the School of Library and Information Studies, Dalhousie University, March 16-17, 1989.* 1990. ISBN 0-7703-9738-7 $11.50.

49. *Peace Information in Canadian Public Libraries*, by Alvin M. Schrader. 1990. ISBN 0-7703-9740-9 $17.50.

50. *The Revolution in New Zealand Librarianship: American Influence as Facilitated by the Carnegie Corporation of New York in the 1930s*, by Maxine K. Rochester. 1990. ISBN 0-7703-9707-7 $14.95.

51. *Atlantic Canadian Literature in English: A Guide to Sources of Information*, by Marilynn J. Rudi. 1991. ISBN 0-7703-9752-2. $17.95

52. *Hardiness, Perseverance and Faith: New Brunswick Library History*, edited by Eric L. Swanick. 1991. ISBN 0-7703-9754-9. $22.95

53. *Directory of Canadian Theatre Archives*, compiled by Heather McCallum and Ruth Pincoe. 1992. ISBN 0-7703-9709-3 $24.95

54. *Information Resource Sharing: Canadian Perspectives*, edited by Carrol D. Lunau. 1993. ISBN 0-7703-9758-1 $19.95

55. *Canadian Business in the Pacific Rim: Selected Information Sources for Canadian Business Professionals*, prepared by Emily Wu and Vivian Howard. 1993. ISBN 0-7703-9760-3 $19.95

56. *Planning for Library Development: Third World Perspectives*, by John Evans. 1995. ISBN 0-7703-9762-X $28.95

57. *Canadiana in United States Repositories: A Preliminary Guide*, by William Gosling. 1994. ISBN 0-7703-9766-2. $26.95